VARIETY

Douglas Maxwell
VARIETY

OBERON BOOKS
LONDON

First published in 2002 by Oberon Books Ltd
Electronic edition published in 2012

Oberon Books Ltd
521 Caledonian Road, London N7 9RH
Tel: 020 7607 3637 / Fax: 020 7607 3629
e-mail: info@oberonbooks.com

A catalogue record for this book is available from the British
Library.

PB ISBN: 978-1-84002-331-2
E ISBN: 978-1-84943-880-3

Cover design: Emma Quinn and Jon Morgan

eBook conversion by Replika Press PVT Ltd, India.

Visit www.oberonbooks.com to read more about all our books
and to buy them. You will also find features, author interviews and
news of any author events, and you can sign up for e-newsletters
so that you're always first to hear about our new releases.

Characters

EDWARD TODD
40s, current manager of the King's

CHARLIE BUCHANAN
20s, a rep from Western Electricals

JACK SALT
40s upwards, the comedian

BETTY KEMBLE
40s, a singer and Jack's wife

CONNOR McNAIR
20s, singer

WALLY / WALLACE / Dr WALFORD CHIPO
20s, novelty act

LORNA SINGH
20s upwards, fortune teller

HARVEY
the theatre's technician

The play is set in The King's Theatre, a medium sized variety theatre somewhere in Scotland. In the past the building has been a busy, but low-class music hall. After a short spell as a legitimate variety theatre, it's on it's last legs. To keep the audience, such as it is, they have been showing films during the concert party bill. However, this week sees the unveiling of their first 'talkie' and the end of live entertainment. From next week on, The King's will become The Regal.

Western Electrical Systems, the company handling the change over, have sent a rep to the theatre to make sure the sound equipment has been installed and that there are no hitches on the horizon.

Variety was first performed at The King's Theatre, Edinburgh on 12 August 2002 as part of the Edinburgh International Festival, as a co-production between EIF and Grid Iron, with the following cast:

DR WALFORD CHIPO, Paul Blair

HARVEY, Jimmy Harrison

CHARLIE BUCHANAN, David Ireland

JACK SALT, John Kazek

EDWARD TODD, Peter Kelly

ROSE, Amy and Sinead Leach

LORNA SINGH, Rina Mahoney

CONNOR MCNAIR, Douglas Rankine

BETTY KEMBLE, Anne Marie Timoney

Director, Ben Harrison

Set Designer, Fred Meller

Lighting Designer, George Tarbuck

Costume Designer, Alice Bee

Composer, Philip Pinsky

Stage Manager, John Cumiskey

Producer, Judith Doherty

Variety was commissioned by Grid Iron with the assistance of the Scottish Arts Council's Playwright Commissions Fund. The production was funded by the City of Edinburgh Council and the Scottish Arts Council, and was sponsored by Lloyds TSB Scotland.

ACT ONE

Scene 1

As the audience move through the foyer into the auditorium to take their seats they feel they are heading into another time. They pass signs around the box office and on the stairs which read: 'Balcony 3/6, Pit 2/-, Upper Circle 1/6, Gallery 1; Another: 'Apprentice Nights Last Thursday of Every Month!'; Another: 'Mind Ye! In the interests of public health this theatre is disinfected with Jeyes Fluid!'

There is no modern music playing – no recorded music at all. Perhaps some musicians from the band are carrying on in the bar. CHARLIE's there. You wouldn't notice him though. He's not the noticeable type. He is wearing a cheap, ill-fitting suit and has his hair plastered down into a centre parting. He's sitting hunched in a corner looking terrified and miserable. Occasionally he may walk about anxiously as if he's looking for somebody. He can't see us. There's a shout from the front of house staff and a bell is rung. Perhaps the audience don't notice the past creeping in like this. Perhaps they do. But what they can't miss, in fact what they can't help tripping over, are sandwich boards with what looks like big news plastered all over them…

GRAND OPENING
THE REGAL
(Formerly The King's Variety Theatre)
Monday 13 Feb 1929
The Most Palatial Cinema
Superlatively Good Entertainment
Exquisitely Upholstered Seats
ALL TALKING!!!
Western Electric System, best quality pictures
Cost to refit £6000!!!!

Not To Be Confused With Cheap Talking Apparatus
SEE & HEAR
'WEARY RIVER'
Richard Barthlemass will thrill you with his stunning
Baritone Voice
They're everywhere: on the walls, behind the bar, in the corri-
dors. This is obviously the big news of the moment. But there's
no time to look at these now. The show is about to start. Some
people might notice that CHARLIE hasn't heard the bell. He's
staying put, deep in thought.

The house lights in the auditorium stay on. There's a dusty
atmosphere. There may be dust sheets draped here and there.
The stage is completely bare and cleared right to the back wall.
At the moment the dominant feature is a large gauze screen
which hangs high, to the side of the stage. It reads:

THREE TIP-TOP A-ONE PICTURES SHOWN WITH
'LEGS LEGS LEGS!!!!!'
A Ticklesome Affair
Jack Salt
'Keep Yer Eye On the Baw!'
& his 'Old Dear'
Betty Kemble
'Accordion/songs/frolics/merriment'
Connor McNair
'Scotland's Gentleman Tenor'
Lorna Singh
'Hoodoo Sorceress'
Dr Walford Chipo
'Equilibrilist/Bloodless Surgery/Buffoonery'
and The Henderson Dancers
'Tartan Tillers!'
ALL NEW SHOW STARTS MONDAY 6 FEBRUARY 1929

It's a variety bill painted in the style of the day. This is a
projection though. Memories and faces, dates and names may
appear on this screen. This is a screen for the past. We'll see

the future later.

With no fanfare or effect in the lighting, a man walks through the stalls and climbs on stage. He looks like someone from the crew, so no-one really takes notice as yet. This is HARVEY. HARVEY is a smallish man dressed all in black who walks with a spring in his step. His wide trousers are held up with a sash and he has a lasso tied to it. He could be mistaken for a dancer or an acrobat or possibly an unusually dapper cowboy. He has big eyes and a childlike quality that's hard to pinpoint. As soon as he makes eye-contact with the audience we begin to quieten. He puts his finger to his lips and speaks directly to us.

HARVEY: Sssssh. Sssssh. If you're quiet you can hear it. Listen. There, do you hear it? Laughter. They say that laughter gets trapped between the walls of a theatre. And they say that when a theatre is torn down and the walls fold into dust, the laughter escapes and sounds out amongst the rubble. But if you listen carefully… listen… you can sometimes catch it while it's trapped; inside the walls, or tied in the folds of the curtains or way, way up, floating next to the highest light. Yes. There it is. Don't be scared. These aren't ghosts…not really. This is a magical place. This is my place. We all have a place like this. A place that we keep in our head, that's part of us and it's safe and strong and magical. Can I ask you something? Can I ask you to think of that place now? Think of your favourite place and who's there with you. Maybe it's the home you grew up in, or maybe it's the place where you first saw the person you're in love with, I don't know. It's your place. Have you got it? Now please, close your eyes.

As the audience close their eyes the lights in the auditorium black out. HARVEY is left in a spotlight. Music starts. A melody in the distance.

Before you open your eyes I want to tell you a secret. You know the place you're thinking of now? *Your* place.

You'll see it again. You will! You'll be back there. How do I know? How can I be sure? Because this, is my place!

The music crescendos and the audience open their eyes to see that a large cinema screen is slowly dropping, filling in the back wall of the stage. HARVEY is excited.

This is my place. This is my house…

The walls are lit.

This is my sky…

The ceiling is lit.

This is my time… And it's all about time. You're not in Edinburgh any more. You're not in Glasgow or London or anywhere glamorous. Oh no. You're somewhere outside the tourist zone. You're in a town away from the lights and the bustle. You're in The King's Variety Theatre on the eleventh of February, 1929. Look at the seats around you. Try to imagine the people who sat there, a century ago. Imagine it. Look at the walls and the ceiling and the seats and let them help you imagine it. It's here. And you can conjure it up if you want. It's right here, trapped in the walls. Time. This is my time. It is a modern time. Every day a new invention. New jobs for people; cars, electrical engineering, plastics, artificial fibres and of course… (*He turns and the screen is lit.*) Talking Pictures! It is a brave time. The war has taught us if we fought for something we could win, so we fought for more. More money, more rights, more freedom, more entertainment. More more more! So it was a time of tide change and retirements. Music Hall thrived on in the cities and down the coast way into the 50s, but here, in the wee places, the old ways didn't stand a chance. The famous names touring the country didn't come here any more. Instead, we had a concert party. (*He goes to the bill.*) The same faces and the same acts, week in week out. But people didn't come to see the acts, not any more. They came to see the screen.

Back to the cinema screen. It flickers to life with a slow 5, 4, 3, 2, 1 countdown and into some grainy 1920s stock footage of a ship. It projects from the centre of the theatre over HARVEY.

We call it cine-variety. Short silent movies and news reels in between the acts. It was the warm up act for Rock'n'Roll and Television. It was the death knell. Last orders at the bar. When talkies arrive, it'll be all over. (*Looks to the bill.*) For all of them. And talkies arrive… today.

The screen flickers off. CHARLIE has entered the auditorium. HARVEY shines a small light on him, which CHARLIE doesn't see. Unlike HARVEY he cannot see the audience. To CHARLIE the theatre is empty. He takes a seat. Looking over his shoulder nervously.

Tomorrow, the King's will become the Regal. And time moves on. For some. Not for me. I'm here again because this is my time. I'm trapped. Something went wrong. I'm here, forever and ever, always trying and always missing. Charlie's nervous. He works for the future. He's here to check the sound equipment for the Regal and get the deeds from Edward, the boss. Edward paces the Gods. One performance to go. An afternoon rehearsal. Jack and Betty, Connor, Wally and Lorna. They don't know anything about Charlie or the Regal. They don't know. And yet they're all here. But we're not. This theatre is empty. We're the shadows this time. We're the ghosts now. We're the laughter in the walls.

The music has continued throughout but now drops to the melody played on an accordion. HARVEY scampers off as we go into total blackout.

Scene 2

When the lights return it is to the stage only. The stage is set to rehearsal lighting. We can now see that it is BETTY who is playing the accordion on stage. JACK is also on stage and is running through their act. JACK is wearing smart trousers and a large comedy hat offset by a very manky looking vest. He looks bored, glancing through bits and pieces of paper and shaking his head. BETTY is wearing a neat twinset and smiling perfectly as if she were mid-performance, but she's drunk. Very drunk. CONNOR sits on the edge of the stage in a very sharp three piece suit, fob, chain and cufflinks. He's looking at sheet music and tapping his foot happily to BETTY's playing. CHARLIE is very, very uncomfortable and terrified of being a nuisance.

The accordion-playing continues for a minute or two. CHARLIE senses it's about to finish and stands up gingerly to clap and ask for Mr Todd. Just as he stands BETTY begins to sing. He rockets back into his seat.

BETTY: (*Singing.*) Me and my man and the moonlight,
　　Struck in the heart by a kiss,
　　A look from my man and I'm alright,
　　On a moonlit night like this.
　　Me and my man and the sunshine
　　Tears in my eyes from a touch
　　I can't believe this fellow's all mine
　　I love my man so much.
　　Me and my man at the seaside…

　　JACK's had enough and interrupts.

JACK: Right, that's enough of that shite. In I come, banter banter banter. Keep yer eye on the baw. Applause. (*Into his 'act' voice.*) Aw no, yer huving me on! The old dear! Applause. Yer huving me on. Old dear, I nearly never recognised you there. Yer fair piling on the beef. Yer so fat these days to get on yer good side I huv to go two streets doon an' turn left. Keep yer eye on the baw!

BETTY: Oh you! I was playing a wee song there.

JACK: I thought I heard folk greetin'. You shouldnae be carrying that thing aboot at your age…

BETTY: Oh you!

JACK: You're so fat…

JACK is interrupted.

The lights blackout and the film is projected over the stage onto the screen.

BETTY shades her eyes and looks out to see what the problem is.

JACK instantly drops his act and roars furiously up to wherever the film is being projected from.

Again, the film is footage of a ship, although now it seems to be sinking.

Aw for the fucking sake of fuck! This is fucking ridiculous, we're trying to fucking rehearse here for fuck sake! How can I fucking get this fucking right with this fucking shite fucking it up every fucking two fucking seconds! Fuck off!

JACK throws his script to the ground.

HARVEY leaps on stage from an impossible position. He jumps from the stage effortlessly and climbs up into the balcony towards the projector and out of sight like spiderman.

BETTY: I don't know what you're moaning about it's the

13

same act we always do, only worse. I don't know why we're even bothering to rehearse it. Today of all days.

JACK: No you don't fucking know do you. It's the lack of decent…fucking…courtesy. It's bad enough I'm on stage with a fucking picture show at all. When I was at the Fucking Empire you didnae get this shite. You're too fucking soft, you let folk walk all over you.

CONNOR: (*Shouting up.*) Problem Tommy?

BETTY: That was Billy.

JACK: There isnae one called Billy.

BETTY: How would you know, you don't give any of them the time of day.

JACK: They aw look fucking identical.

CONNOR: Problem Billy?

Suddenly the sound switches on. It's a dramatic commentary of the sinking ship footage in a huge American accent. This shocks the performers beyond belief. Terror.

WALLY and LORNA appear like ghosts on the stage, staring out as if they've been summoned. WALLY is in a cheap suit and LORNA is in a glamorous sari. It's obvious they have not been told about the talkies coming.

VOICE: 'Hundreds of shocked and terrified passengers stare with disbelief as their craft which moments earlier held them safely to its bosom, is now sucked to its watery destiny beneath the fickle waves and cruel pounding of God's most fearsome creation…the ocean.'

The sound stops, followed by the picture spinning and then blinking off. The players remain in their shocked and terrified tableau.

JACK: That was a talkie. A fucking talkie! What's the

score? Where's that fucking lunatic Todd? (*Screaming to the Gods.*) Todd! I know you're up there, wandering about like the fucking phantom of the opera. You're meant to be in fucking charge here! (*To the others.*) He's fucking mad. He's a fucking broomstick.

CONNOR: Now come on Jack, he's a very sick man.

CHARLIE is stewing in his own nervousness now and can see no way out except to identify himself. He stands up and moves to the stage and is about to speak when JACK spots him.

JACK: I'm a fucking sick man. Sick of all this shite. (*Shouting up again.*) Now listen to me Todd, I'm Jack Salt and I don't like to be surprised…(*Surprised.*) Aaaah! Who the fuck is that? (*Pointing at CHARLIE.*)

The players gather on the edge of the stage staring at him.

CHARLIE: I… I… I… I… I…

HARVEY appears from somewhere above holding a spotlight which he shines on CHARLIE with delight.

HARVEY: Hello chap.

JACK: I said, who…the…fuck…is *that*?

CHARLIE: I… I… I… I… I…

HARVEY: Are you Charlie Buchanan chap?

CHARLIE: I…Charles…actually…Mr…yes Charlie Buchanan that's me.

JACK: And what the fuck are you doing here apart from sneaking about and stuttering?

BETTY: Mind your own business you.

JACK: This is my fucking business.

BETTY: Everyone knows about your business. Except me.

Or maybe I do. She's young, I'll give you that.

JACK: (*To CHARLIE.*) Are you the new manager? Are we getting talkies? Are we getting the sack?

HARVEY: (*To CHARLIE.*) Mr Todd wants to speak to you chap.

CHARLIE: Ah…righto…good…em…yes…I have an eh… appointment.

HARVEY: Nervous chap?

CHARLIE: No. Well…no. I've done this type of thing…oh countless.

JACK: (*To HARVEY.*) So what's he saying about all this talkie business?

HARVEY: Who?

JACK: Captain fucking Ahab!

HARVEY: He's coming down. The rest of you have to break until Enter The Villagers.

CONNOR: Is he alright?

HARVEY: He's coming down chap. To see Charlie.

This gets a reaction. Obviously CHARLIE should feel honoured but it only adds to his terror.

Break everyone. Clear the stage.

CONNOR: Actually, while we're all here could we quickly sort out this business with the chimp?

JACK: What fucking business with the chimp? What fucking chimp? What fucking…*what?*

CONNOR: Well, long story short, my sports jacket has gone missing and it was last seen being taken from my dressing room by a chimp of all things. Trouble is, there's quite a bit of money missing from my wallet. The chimp may have taken it to eat, or, worst case scenario, to spend.

HARVEY: There's no chimps in this building chap. Edward wouldn't allow it. Not after that bear act from Russia attacked the orchestra.

CONNOR: Yes, poor old Maureen. She was the best orchestra we've ever had.

JACK: I told him. Bear act! There's no such thing. A bear act's just a bear with a fucking idiot tied to it.

CONNOR: (*Continuing regardless.*) Anyway, I'd say at a guesstimate he, or she, would be about yay high. (*Holds his hand out at about three feet off the ground.*) Correct Wally?

WALLY: (*Uncomfortable.*) Yeah, yeah whatever. I dunno. Maybe taller.

CONNOR: Maybe taller! Did you hear that everyone, 'maybe taller'. So what we're dealing with here is a taller than average chimp with an eye for the finer things in life.

JACK: Ah fuck this for a game of soldiers. (*To CHARLIE.*) What's the story you? Are we getting the sack?

BETTY: Does it matter? We've been finished for years.

JACK: Ach Betty shut up. Just remember who's at the top of the fucking bill here.

BETTY: Aye, the pictures.

JACK: Naw, me. (*Threateningly.*) Keep yer eye on the baw.

CONNOR: Actually, would everyone mind taking their eye *off* the ball just until we get this chimp matter settled. Okydokey then, perhaps if we split into groups and had a quick look round…

WALLY: (*Shouting.*) Just leave it will you! Nobody's interested in this bloody chimp.

CONNOR: (*Concerned.*) Okay mate, steady on. Are you alright?

WALLY: No…I'm…it's just it might not have been a chimp.

CONNOR: You said it was a chimp.

WALLY: I know but, it was dark. I didn't know you'd make such a big deal out of it.

CONNOR: What are you saying Wally? If it wasn't a chimp what was it? Some kind of…monkeyboy?

WALLY: No, I'm not saying it was a monkeyboy…well I don't know. (*To CONNOR.*) All I'm saying is don't make such a big deal about stuff. You're always making a big deal out of stuff. (*Dramatically.*) You're so damn… *dramatic!*

CONNOR: Here listen, I'm sorry Wally I didn't mean to upset you.

CONNOR goes to touch WALLY who pulls back sharply.

WALLY: Don't touch me.

Pause.

HARVEY: I'm sure the wallet will turn up chap.

CONNOR: Ach aye, no doubt. These things always do. It's just that it was money I'd made from a special charity gala. For the wives of men killed down the mines. I was to hand it over at a dinner on Monday. Would've been nice to give something back.

JACK: Here we fucking go.

CONNOR: (*Sarcastic.*) Oh sorry to interrupt this very important work we're doing here, with idle chat of the common man.

JACK: Bugger the common man to fuck.

CONNOR: Yes. And bugger their thirteen per cent pay decrease. And bugger the fact they come in here night after night paying what pittance they do have on us.

JACK: Fucking up my timing with all that coughing.

CONNOR: And bugger the fact they actually do a man's job. (*With disgust.*) While we do *this*. Edward understands. He says I should sing Labour songs in my act. (*A look to WALLY.*) Maybe that's what's missing. A connection to the real world.

WALLY: You can't change your act without my say so. It's in your contract remember Connor.

CONNOR: Edward was keen. He led the Variety walkout of '17. Very political wasn't he Betty?

A sad nod from BETTY.

JACK: Aye but he's mad now so all bets are off.

BETTY: Convenient that.

WALLY: And your contract's not with Edward. It's with me.

CONNOR: (*Instantly backing down.*) Of course. The contract. Maybe the money will turn up.

All eyes go immediately to WALLY.

HARVEY: (*To WALLY and with venom.*) As I say, I'm absolutely certain it'll turn up.

CONNOR: Well. I hope so.

Pause.

BETTY: Does anyone want to know why I'm drunk?

JACK: The sun came up.

BETTY: It's an anniversary.

Some 'Happy Anniversary's from people, but everyone's embarrassed.

It's not *our* anniversary.

Pause.

JACK: (*Hasn't heard the above.*) What were we talking about before aw this fucking shite? Oh aye! (*To CHARLIE.*) You. Sap. Are we all getting the boot or what? Are the talkies coming?

CHARLIE: Em…well…obviously…em…there's one or two…what with…as Arthur always says…

JACK: (*Spelling it out as if to a simpleton.*) Who…are… you…and…what…the…fuck…is…going…on?

Pause.

CHARLIE looks at everyone and decides the time has come to be strong.

CHARLIE: I'm in the picture business.

CHARLIE looks out into the auditorium. There's a beat. CHARLIE faints.

No-one moves. They all look at CHARLIE who lies on the stage as if it's an act he does. LORNA goes over to him and kneels down.

JACK: Keep away fae him ya wog.

CONNOR: Jack!

JACK: She'll be going through his pockets. Wog tinker…

bloody…jiggaboo.

*LORNA turns and stares at JACK. There is a very odd
moment between them.*

HARVEY disappears, making his way to the stage.

WALLY: The picture business? Oh my God.

JACK: Eh?

WALLY: (*Guiltily.*) Nothing. No nothing. Let me in to him
please.

JACK: Why should we fucking let *you* in?

BETTY: Is he dead? Get one of the Harvey brothers,
they'll know what to do.

JACK: (*Still to WALLY.*) Ho! Who made you the boss?

CONNOR: (*Shouting out into the auditorium and where
HARVEY used to be.*) Bobby! Billy! Tommy! Eh…is there
a Harry? Harry! Richard! Richard!

BETTY: There isnae one called Richard.

WALLY: Give him space to breathe. Back away.

JACK: Don't fucking listen to him. Close in!

WALLY: I'm a doctor!

JACK: No you're fucking not.

WALLY: Read the bill. Doctor Walford Chipo. Doctor!

CONNOR: Yes but Wallace old son, you're not *actually* a
doctor.

WALLY: Read the bill Connor, 'Doctor'!

*LORNA stands and waves her arms. They fan away
from her. She goes back to CHARLIE mumbling
something under her breath. He wakes up. Looking*

straight into LORNA's eyes. He's stunned.

WALLY: See. Who's the doctor now?

JACK: Not you ya…

CONNOR: Are you alright Charlie? You had a wee spell.

CHARLIE: It was all the people. I looked out at all the seats and suddenly there were faces looking back at me. Hundreds of faces. Like ghosts. (*To LORNA.*) Who are you?

LORNA smiles at CHARLIE, frowns at everyone else, and then exits. She passes HARVEY entering as she goes.

JACK: It's that stinking wog's fault we're in this fucking mess.

CONNOR: Oh for goodness sake.

JACK: She fucking cursed this place. You all heard her. After that night. She cursed this building and everyone in it. And now look at us.

HARVEY: Are you okay chap?

CHARLIE: I don't know what happened.

HARVEY: It's the only time I've ever heard of anyone getting stage fright in an empty theatre.

CHARLIE: The camera! Is the camera alright?

WALLY: Camera?

HARVEY: The projector. It's a camera too. Yes chap it's swell don't worry.

WALLY: (*Conspiratorially.*) Here Connor, quick word.

WALLY exits in a hurry.

CONNOR reluctantly follows. He pats BETTY on the shoulder.

CONNOR: Chin up.

She forces a lame smile.

CONNOR exits.

JACK: What are those fucking jolly boys up to?

BETTY: (*To JACK.*) You've forgotten everything haven't you? Every single thing.

JACK: Eh?

BETTY: From the day we met until now. It's all worthless to you. But you never forget about the future do you? Paranoid that your time in the spotlight's nearly up. Well it's here. It's arrived. Maybe now it's time to look back.

JACK: Are you telling me they're up to something. Is that it? Plotting against me?

BETTY: Jack.

JACK: What? (*Pause.*) Ach Betty I don't have time for your drama. I'm top of the bill here I've got to worry about my fucking career.

BETTY: I was top of the bill once. At The Alhambra. When you were still getting the bird at bursts in the Panoptican. Do you remember that?

JACK: Away you go and get changed for Enter The Villagers. I'm going to see what they're up to.

BETTY: If I step off this stage will you follow me?

JACK: Sssh!

JACK sneaks off to eavesdrop on WALLY and CONNOR.

BETTY: (*To herself.*) A trapeze artist once told me that the only way she could pluck up the courage to make the leap, is to convince herself that she didn't want to be caught. Once she had that in her head, she could do anything. I wish I could be that brave. I need to be pushed.

BETTY steps off the stage and exits through the audience.

Scene 3

CHARLIE is sitting up. Feeling his head for injuries. HARVEY is somewhere. When he speaks to the audience CHARLIE can't see him.

HARVEY: (*To audience.*) Show people always keep one eye on the wings; dreading the moment they see their replacement waiting nervously in the shadows. They'll be younger, newer, fresher, different. Maybe you know the feeling? Maybe you've suddenly found that the act you use to get through life doesn't quite work anymore. It's time to leave the stage. You're old now. Or maybe you're the new blood? Maybe you've felt that prickly annoyance at the old ways. You can hardly wait to walk into the light and take over. You're young. And so it rolls on. This bill is always changing.

CHARLIE sees HARVEY.

CHARLIE: I feel like an idiot.

HARVEY: No need chap.

CHARLIE: (*Angry at himself.*) Imagine fainting. I…couldn't help it.

HARVEY: You don't strike me as a show person Charlie am I right?

CHARLIE: I was very nearly a priest.

HARVEY: What happened?

CHARLIE: I got scared. I fainted then too actually. All my family were there. When I came to they didn't like me anymore. I'm such a coward.

HARVEY: We're all cowards sometimes. Even me. (*Has a think about whether we should say this, but CHARLIE looks so helpless.*) One time, me and the brothers had an interview for a job at the Empire...

CHARLIE: The brothers?

HARVEY: My brothers. Tommy, Jimmy, Andy, Billy and Richard. We do all the technical stuff in the hall. We're the blood in the veins of the building Edward says. We do the tabs, the limes, the pictures. Edward had pulled some strings and got us a meeting with the DSM of the Empire up in Glasgow. Now, the Empire boys are the best in the business. They rig the lights with lassoes and dance over cables so it was our big chance. Our only ambition.

CHARLIE: But you didn't get the job?

HARVEY: No. (*Ashamed.*) We went all the way up to Glasgow, and then sat in a pub across from the theatre, watching the clock roll on while we stayed put.

CHARLIE: You didn't even go in?

HARVEY: No.

Now it's HARVEYs turn to look down. He starts to twirl his lasso looking up into the darkness above the stage.

HARVEY: We're still here. We're all cowards sometimes. Our lassos are just for show. But one day I'll swoop in with my lasso and everything'll be different. I practise it. I'll be an Empire Boy one day. (*HARVEY snaps out of it.*) Now here, I've no told anyone that. I tell folk that we turned the job down.

CHARLIE: I won't say.

HARVEY: That's right, priests aren't allowed to spread about people's confessions are they?

CHARLIE: Well…no. But I'm not a priest.

HARVEY: So you *are* going to spread it about?

CHARLIE: No!

HARVEY: Well…okay then, you have to tell me something so we're even. Something secret.

HARVEY's swinging his lasso again.

CHARLIE: Something secret? I don't really… (*CHARLIE looks round the theatre and is reminded of something horrible*) When I was wee a comic picked on me. It was the worst thing ever. I've never been back to a show since. I've never been back in a hall until today. That's why I love pictures. You can fade into the dark and they'll never pick on you. I thought that working for a cinema company would be like working in pictures, away from the real world, but it's not. I get picked on in there too. The only reason I'm here today is that everyone else in the office is at Arthur's daughter's wedding. Arthur's the boss and he's a mean wee swine. He's so mean! His daughter's getting married to this guy called Hendry and he hates me too. He steals my ideas and spreads lies about me around the office so I never get promoted. Fiona's dead nice. Too nice for Hendry. I wrote her a letter once.

HARVEY: Ended in tears did it?

CHARLIE: My squint nearly came back.

HARVEY sees something. He puts his fingers to his lips and then throws the lasso offstage. There's a scream. He viciously drags WALLY onto the stage.

WALLY is holding a sports jacket and he's furious.

WALLY: How dare you! How very, very dare you ya filthy curtain monkey. Let me go.

WALLY struggles out of the lasso and shoots to his feet, smoothing his hair and smiling at CHARLIE as if nothing were wrong.

Ha ha ha, the sheer camaraderie of the theatre, Mr Buchanan, if you bottle it…

HARVEY: What you doing sneaking about? Is that Connor's jacket?

WALLY: Shouldn't you be away pulling on a rope?

HARVEY: I'm watching you. We all are. You're ruining that boy. Connor's got a big future and he could do without the likes of you dragging him down. He could be the next Lauder. You're on a warning.

WALLY: *I'm* on a warning? You're the one attacking people. I'm telling Edward. Which one are you?

HARVEY: I'm not saying.

WALLY: I'll report you all then. I'm the talent.

HARVEY: Pfft. (*To CHARLIE.*) I take it you'll want to check The Rotornaught 60?

CHARLIE: The projector. Well…I don't really know anything about it. He says I've to use it to film tonight to show at next weeks opening, but can that be right.

HARVEY: Oh aye it's right. All these old cameras can project. I'd've thought he'd want a newer version for the talkies but it's his money I suppose.

CHARLIE: He's so mean it's dangerous.

HARVEY: So it might not work but I'll do my best chap. Stay here and Eddie'll find you. (*To WALLY.*) Careful you.

WALLY: (*Sneering.*) You're going to rue this moment. I'm on my way up. (*Nudges CHARLIE.*) Right? And I'm going to expose this racket you and your phantom brothers have got going. Never seen in the same room Mr Buchanan. This mouth-breathing gibbon's getting five pay packets for himself I know he is. There are no brothers!

HARVEY: (*With threat for WALLY's sake.*) Be careful when you're walking round the theatre Charlie. You could trip, things can fall, people can deliberately swing things at you. (*Grabbing the jacket from WALLY.*) I'll give this back to Connor shall I?

WALLY: I found it.

HARVEY exits. When he's gone:

You're dismissed! (*To CHARLIE.*) Alone at last. You'll've been wondering where I'd got to. Well I'm here now you can relax.

CHARLIE: (*Confused.*) Oh good.

WALLY: Feeling a bit better, swell. It was the least I could do, being the resident doctor and all.

CHARLIE: Oh I see.

WALLY: Thanks for keeping this all hush hush.

CHARLIE: Well…

WALLY: Only I feel some of the, shall we say, less good acts, would probably feel threatened by the process.

CHARLIE: Would they?

WALLY: The older ones yes. It's hard for some people to accept that they haven't got 'it' you see. They act up.

CHARLIE: Do they?

WALLY: Almost constantly. I'm Dr Walford Chipo by the way. Equilibrilist and electronic magician. Although I'm sure you're more familiar with my old self, Dunlop? From McNair and Dunlop? It was a few years ago now but we're still talked about in some circles. I represent Connor McNair the tenor by the way. Known him since we were wee. Write his material. So if it's him you fancy you'll have to deal with me. He's old hat though. Popular with the old dears maybe but not what you'd call talkie material eh?

He laughs loudly.

CHARLIE tries to join in but is too confused.

But as I say, I'm his manager so you would deal with me. Same as with all the acts. Well…aye. Or maybe it'll be me that takes your fancy? Eh? Stranger things have happened. Connor's not…he's not that good.

CHARLIE: You're his manager?

WALLY: You know I write so many letters. 'Please come! Give me a chance!' (*Laughs desperately.*) I'd almost forgotten about it. Are you using the film to make your decision? Swell idea. Cos some acts that are good on stage may not be good on screen. And vice versa. But you know that already. You're wise.

CHARLIE: Am I?

WALLY: So wise. Think about it, everyone else is at the big halls looking for the next Chaplin or Dot Arnold or Harry Lauder. But you're here. Off the beaten track. You're wise.

CHARLIE: I think you might be getting me mixed up.

WALLY: Oh no. You're wise alright. Wise to the whole shakedown. Listen…(*In whispers.*) I also represent Helen Henderson, the dancer. Know what I mean?

CHARLIE: You mean…?

WALLY: No. I mean rep-re-sent. I'm not bribing you. It's not a bribe but it's there if you're up to it. She's a swell gal. Listen I'm not sure it's such a good idea to tell Todd what's going on, it may just tip him over the edge. He's heading for the laughing academy as it is. Just pretend you're here to check the projector or something. Okay? Remember, talk to me before you approach any of the acts. We've got an understanding.

WALLY shakes CHARLIE's hand for a long, long time. Then suddenly, like an animal in a forest, he gets spooked and exits quickly into the wings. EDWARD is coming. Maybe we can see JACK scampering away too. He's been listening in.

Scene 4

Music. The whole building seems to change complexion. The bill fades away on the gauze screen. The screen glows. The theatre is ill. CHARLIE is stranded centre stage and is getting scared again.

CHARLIE: Mr Todd? Are you there?

CHARLIE's eye catches something move in a box. It's EDWARD. He's a small man in his middle age. He wears three piece suit with a fob and chain, but his collar has been wrenched open and his face is flushed. He has a moustache and a wild, sad look in his eye. He's the captain of a sinking ship and he's decided to go down at the helm. He's loosing his grip. He can see things and when he sees things we see things. It's like he can control the building. He's dying. If he can't be seen, and maybe even if he can, he climbs onto the edge of the box. Sometimes he talks to CHARLIE, sometimes he directs his speech out to the theatre, but he can't see us.)

EDWARD: (*Sings.*)

Every road thro' life is a long, long road,
Fill'd with joys and sorrows too,

As you journey on, how your heart will yearn,
For the things most dear to you.
With wealth and love 'tis so
But onward we must go.

Keep right on to the end of the road, keep right on till
the end,
Tho' the way be long, let your heart be strong, keep
right round the bend.
Tho' you're tired and weary still journey on, till you
come to your happy abode,
Where all you love you've been dreaming of will be
there…
At the end of the road.

*He closes his eyes lost in a spell. A faint picture of
HARRY LAUDER appears on the screen.*

He's coming! The rafters will be rocked, the standing
room jammed and all troubles thrown to the wind. 'All
the love I've been dreaming of.' Harry Lauder is on his
way! Can you believe it Mr Buchanan? Harry Lauder
is coming here! Tonight. There were times, oh sir there
were times when I lay awake sweating it out. 'Todd' I'd
say, 'Oh Todd you're budgeting on magic. Tell the players that the theatre is shutting and give them a chance!'
But there was always a voice, a tiny song, a melody in
my head which said that magic would arrive and save
the day. And it's arrived. (*Producing a well thumbed piece
of paper. It's a letter*) Harry Lauder will sing here tonight
and the building will live on! Resurrected. I thought
he'd forgotten me. Maybe I was just another face in another crowd from years ago. But no. He remembers me.
(*Reading.*) 'Mr Lauder understands…' He understands!
He'll sing here tonight and the crowds will return and
you and your (*Spits the word.*) *business* will have to go
elsewhere.

A little girl wearing a white coat walks slowly on the stage behind CHARLIE. EDWARD looks at her spellbound not listening to CHARLIE. He holds out a hand to her. CHARLIE can't see her. The girl can't see either of them. During CHARLIE's next line she walks across the stage and exits and EDWARD snaps out of it.

CHARLIE: You haven't told them that the theatre is shutting? But what'll they do? We take over tomorrow. Harry Lauder can't stop Arthur. This building is going to be a cinema next week.

EDWARD: There are souls here, Mr Buchanan. Small splitters of souls given away in coughs of laughter and drops of tears. Given by the people to the building. It collects them, it lacquers the walls with them, it guilds it's statues with them. They're immortal. That can't just *stop* can it? Human beings entertaining other human beings. I used to think that was a constant. That it was a *necessity* even. But now I'm not so sure. Perhaps we don't need other people at all? Do we prefer to watch from afar or on a screen? Can an entire art form, all those souls, just *stop*? I'm dying Mr Buchanan. I'm ill beyond sympathy. I used to paint but now I'm blind. I used to play the fiddle but now my finger tips are numb. I used to be happy. My talents are seeping away. My soul is too. Out into the building. And the iller I get, the iller the building gets. I suppose eventually I'll kill it. But it will be a joint suicide, a lovers pact. It will be pathetic.

EDWARD ducks out of sight, upset.

CHARLIE: Em…are you alright? I take it Arthur spoke to you about the deeds. I really just have to pick them up, check the camera for tonight and then I'll be out of your hair. Hello? Is Harry Lauder really coming here? You wouldn't think he'd have time for a place like…

EDWARD appears down at stage level, although he's not really speaking to CHARLIE. He's talking to himself. As he describes the theatre he gestures wildly, conducting the change.

EDWARD: This theatre cost nineteen thousand to build in 1904. It grew upwards from a pub. In those days the shape of the auditorium was very different to this, of course. It really was just a hall. No rake to the seats, a bar at the back, pies served on trays throughout, men standing around all sides. It was a rough house for rough people.

There's the roar of a rowdy audience. EDWARD paces the stage like a comedian, CHARLIE is forced to sit on the edge of the stage.

They didn't even dim the lights when the acts came on, if you can imagine.

He doesn't need to. The house lights return but in a low unnatural colour. The roar of chatter gets so loud EDWARD has to shout.

The boys would shower whelks and sprays of undesirable liquids upon the acts they didn't take to.

EDWARD ducks as If getting pissed on.

Women were not allowed in unaccompanied, due to the type of lady who would frequent the hall in those days. Dan Leno played here with his brothers and was literally pulled offstage by the owner.

EDWARD ducks out the way of a large hook that appears at the side of the stage. There is a picture of Dan Leno on the gauze screen. The picture changes to a selection of music hall interiors.

Then came a change in licensing laws, 1917. No food no drink, no undesirable sprays. Music halls were now to be called Variety Theatres and this place got a re-fit to suit it's sudden rise in class.

The house lights dim, there's period music. As right at the beginning the walls and ceiling of the theatre are lit.

And yet somehow, I pine for the rougher days. I see soldiers with their red uniforms and their Victorian ladies, and the smell of the food and the smoke and the noise and the uproar.

And so do we. A soldier and his girlfriend sit in a box, laughing and applauding silently. It seems smoky and the laughter in the walls return, along with the clatter of a rough audience.

But the uproar has gone.

It all disappears. EDWARD stands in a single spotlight.

At first we attracted the biggest names who were touring the country on ever changing bills. With each Monday, a new poster brought a victory.

The following faces appear on the screen. EDWARD speaks these names with reverence.

Mckenzie Murdoch, Fred Karno, Jack Lorimer, WF Frame, Will Fyffe. They had them standing at the windows, desperate for scraps. Happy for Tabs. They were so good. So good. But God almighty…times change.

Due to public demand, a year ago, we installed a screen to show short films throughout the show.

The cinema screen flickers to life.

Big houses again. But it's not fair. It's an uneven bill. And now of course the Talkies have arrived and the curtain must drop completely.

Turning and shouting at the screen.

No more. I order you to stop! Stop!

It doesn't. EDWARD's on his knees. The little girl from before enters and skips off the stage and out the door to the auditorium.

Rose! It's me. I'm sorry.

The screen goes off. EDWARD slumps. Resigned.

Mind you, I've seen some beautiful things. Houdini being carried shoulder high. A finale delayed for an hour as the audience presented the performers with gifts. Harry Lauder on a street corner singing for a group of soldiers who'd spotted him walking by. Standing ovation after standing ovation. But it's laughter in the walls now Mr Buchanan, laughter in the walls.

Seriously, to CHARLIE.

But what if I'm just pretending? What if all this blather is just a way of dodging the blame? Maybe I'm pleading insanity? (*Turning on CHARLIE.*) Or maybe I'm simply trying to scare you away? Are you scared Mr Buchanan? Scared enough to turn around and leave us be? I can't let you take this building son. I can't. I'm here to stop you. One way or another. Harry's coming tonight… (*Looks at the letter.*)…he is…but if not…I can't let you be the one to end it. It should come from my hands.

He leaps to his feet with a mad energy.

I'll tear down this theatre brick by brick and set all the souls free. I'll pull down the curtains and smash the lights. I'll roll the carpets and I'll take a sledge hammer to the stage. When it's all gone I will be too. And maybe that's for the best. I'll start with the new and finish with the old. The projector! I'm going to sacrifice it for the greater good.

Sings as he runs backstage. We can hear his song travel into the distance.

Tho' you're tired and weary still journey on, till you come to your happy abode,
Where all you love you've been dreaming of will be there…
At the end of the road!

Scene 5

CHARLIE: (*It dawns on him.*) Wait a minute. Mr Todd! What do you mean 'sacrifice' the projector? I'm almost certain Arthur would be against sacrificing on any level.

CHARLIE is beginning to panic and scuttles round a bit, headless chicken-style.

Em…Humphrey! Tony! Archie! Em…Philip!

HARVEY appears from somewhere ridiculous.

HARVEY: Help you chap?

CHARLIE: It's Mr Todd. I think he's going to smash up the projector.

HARVEY: Have we met?

CHARLIE: He says he's going to take a sledge hammer… have we met? Of course we've met.

HARVEY: No you see that'll be Tommy. I'm not Tommy. Tommy's taller than me. Was he taller than me?

CHARLIE: Well…

HARVEY: So Edward's going to smash the projector eh? And that would be bad because?

CHARLIE: Because Arthur would kill me. It's the only thing I have to do. Apart from pick up the deeds…ah dammit I haven't done that either. Is there anyway to stop him?

HARVEY: You're being a bit dramatic chap, if you don't mind me saying. Aye. I'll ask him not to do it. That might work. Did he go the back way?

CHARLIE points to where EDWARD exited.

Then I'll take the high road.

HARVEY jumps off the stage and makes his way to the projector, disappearing from view.

CHARLIE realises he's alone on stage. He suddenly feels incredibly self conscious.

CHARLIE: (*To wherever HARVEY went.*) Is there an office I could maybe wait in? Or a waiting room? I don't really feel…comfortable… I…

There's a rumbling noise from backstage. The sound of an audience roaring with laughter is heard through the walls. CHARLIE looks terror-stricken. He seems to shrink. He's getting younger and younger. The gauze screen changes to a poster for a show called 'Funtime!' at The Empire, Glasgow. The rumbling turns into a stomp. Like a giant approaching. CHARLIE turns to face the back of the stage. Music is heard, although it's distorted. The lights change, again they are distorted in some way. A huge shadow is cast from behind the cinema screen. We hear a voice:

VOICE: Any of the boys and girls? Put up your hand and shout 'me'!

We hear hundreds of children screaming 'Me!'

Humble bumble trips and treats, the child that Uncle wants to meet is…you!

The cinema screen rises and standing behind it is a giant. He's a COMEDIAN and he has picked CHARLIE to join him on stage. He is huge and monstrous; CHARLIE's hellish memory. CHARLIE is now nine years old and in the correct proportions next to the giant COMEDIAN. He's delighted to have been picked. He's nervous still but waves at his mum out there in the stalls. Maybe the COMEDIAN's voice is recorded and warped.

COMEDIAN: And what's your name?

CHARLIE: Charlie.

COMEDIAN: Charlie. Charlie's Aunt! Well Auntie's no here the day Charlie boy so do you want to help Uncle out?

CHARLIE: Yes. I want to be you when I grow up.

Big laughs.

CHARLIE smiles at the response.

COMEDIAN: Ha! You want to be me? You'd make a good comic. Do you know why?

CHARLIE: (*Delighted.*) Why?

COMEDIAN: Cos you've got the worst squint I've ever seen! Squinto. One eye looking for ye the other looking by ye.

CHARLIE's face drops. He looks out mortified at the audience who are hooting with laughter.

You wouldnae need make-up wi a coupon like that! Am I right ladies and gentlemen? Ha ha ha! Eyes like fried eggs on a sinking ship.

CHARLIE: (*Tiny.*) It's getting better.

COMEDIAN: Oh c'mon Squinty ye huv tae learn tae take a joke if ye want to be a comic.

CHARLIE's face screws up. He cries.

Aw are you scared of all the people staring at you? Hundreds of faces. But it must look double the amount to you eh? No that's no fair. Here Squinter, a bit of advice. I don't think show business is for you. You should be a priest. Cos you'll never get a girl wi a face like that!

The laughs from the audience magnify and get distorted.

CHARLIE is crying and drops to his knees with his head in his hands, turning back into himself.

The giant COMEDIAN takes a bow.

The cinema screen is slowly dropping over him.

Thank you very much! Ha ha! KEEP YER EYE ON THE BAW!!!

These last words echo as if in an empty theatre again. CHARLIE is an adult and snaps out of it. He spins round to where the COMEDIAN was. It's just the screen. The lights return to their previous state. CHARLIE stands. He's put two and two together. The comic that picked on him and ruined his life happens to have been JACK. CHARLIE wants revenge. He exits backstage.

Scene 6

During HARVEY's speech we may see EDWARD slowly killing his building. We may see BETTY drinking alone, lost in a horrible memory. But what we definitely see is a strange silent moment between JACK and LORNA. It's an intimate moment but not sexual. A strange closeness. HARVEY is sadder than before.

HARVEY: You're grabbing and groping, trying to keep things together but no-matter how hard you try the tide keeps coming and coming and soon everything is washing away from you, through your fingers and out into the world. You can swim and zoom along with current. You can tread the water and observe the flood. Or you can drown. But no-matter what you do or how hard you fight when the tide changes, some things will get lost forever. (*The building.*) This will all go. And everyone who played in it and everyone who laughed in it will go. And *we'll* all go. This night won't even be a memory. It'll be lost, forever. But we all know this. I think we're born with a feeling of loss. The feeling that whatever came before us is somehow better than what we have now. And no-matter when we come in, we feel that we've missed the best part of the show and lost something important which we can't put a name to.

Scene 7

The players have gathered to discuss some big news. WALLY and JACK are having a fight, BETTY and LORNA sit together quietly and CONNOR is trying to keep the peace.

CONNOR: And you're sure you haven't made a mistake?

WALLY: The only mistake anyone's made is Jack thinking it's him he's here to see.

JACK: Of course he's fucking here to see me ya fuck pole. I'm top of the fucking bill.

WALLY: You're past it. You're finished. Oh what? Are you shocked to hear the truth? Well that's what happens when you eavesdrop on *private conversations!*

JACK: (*Beat.*) And what was all that shite you told him about being everyone's manager? *That* isnae true.

CHARLIE has entered from somewhere. No-one can see him except LORNA. CHARLIE hears the following and at first is shocked, but still burning from his encounter with the giant he decides to be bold.

WALLY: (*To everyone and with quick desperation.*) Listen, I've been lucky enough to pull a few strings and get Buchanan down here to see me, talk through contracts and my options and so on. I organised it. I'm his connection here. He specifically asked for me. Now, I represent Connor and if the rest of you are wise you'll let me handle things for you. I'm the only one that he'll deal with. I'm your only chance to get out of here. The talkies are in. Ask yourself this: what happens next?

Pause.

JACK: And you know all about film contracts and all that fucking shite?

WALLY: Of course.

CONNOR: But Wally...are you sure?

WALLY: All contracts are basically...

CONNOR: No, I mean are you sure he's the man from RKO?

WALLY: (*To CONNOR, coolly.*) Stupid old Wally eh? Daft old Wally who fails at everything must have got it wrong. How could that idiot Wallace have organised this eh? You're so used to being the one who... I actually have a few skills of my own you know...

CONNOR: I know.

WALLY: You're so caught up in yourself. Just cos a couple of old ladies like a sing-a-long you think you're Harry Lauder. Well I have a few skills...

CONNOR: I know.

WALLY: We used to be…we used to be a team.

CONNOR: I know I'm sorry Wally.

WALLY: Just because this is my chance. My chance for a change. I've been waiting all my life for this.

CONNOR: No-one thinks more of you than I do. Me and you. The old act. I…I just don't want you to get your hopes dashed. (*Sadly.*) I know what that's like.

BETTY: (*Drunk in a minor key and to herself.*) So what does happen next?

CONNOR: Sorry pet?

BETTY: What does happen next? What happens to us? Next?

JACK: She's fucking tight. In her cups. Today of all days.

BETTY: (*Shouts.*) TODAY OF ALL DAYS!

JACK: Aye, today of all days! The one time a fucking talent scout arrives and you're blootered. Selfish fucking bitch. No any old talent scout either, fucking pictures. You know how much I fucking want this. That's why you've done it, to fucking scupper me. Well don't think I'm letting you talk to him. (*Awkward.*) Wally…you can…you can organise my side too.

WALLY: Thank you Jack. Happy to. If I may say so you're exactly the type of act that he'll be looking for. And the rest of you should follow suit if you know what's good for you.

BETTY: I haven't got a clue what's good for me.

JACK: And don't think you're going on. You're not fucking up my act.

BETTY: I'm your wife.

JACK: Today of all days.

WALLY: And remember to be friendly. Don't mention that you know he's from Hollywood. Just smile and say, 'How do you do Mr Buchanan.'

CONNOR: (*Seeing CHARLIE.*) Oh hello Mr Buchanan.

WALLY: No I think 'How do you do' is better.

CONNOR: (*Pointing at where CHARLIE is entering from.*) No I mean…

They all turn to see CHARLIE.

CHARLIE looks nervous.

JACK: I'm no fucking saying fucking…(*Sees CHARLIE.*) Ahhh! Stop fucking doing that ya wee fucking…I mean…how…fucking…do you do?

EVERYONE: (*Except LORNA and with varying enthusiasm.*) How do you do Mr Buchanan.

CHARLIE: (*Tiny.*) Fine.

WALLY: I've lined up quite a show for you Mr Buchanan. (*Winks.*)

CHARLIE looks at their faces and feels he has to tell the truth, about the theatre shutting and his job.

CHARLIE: Look, I'm sorry. For you all. You see Mr Todd should've told you something. Something about what… he's lost.

JACK: He's lost his fucking mind. That's fucking clear.

CHARLIE: So I think I should tell you the truth.

BETTY: Oh no darling, we don't tell the truth here.

JACK: Just fucking ignore her. She's not in the act. She's… ignore her. What were you saying?

CHARLIE sees the look on BETTY's face. And remembers.

CHARLIE: I think I've seen you before?

JACK: Oh aye?

CHARLIE: Yes…em…you were at the Empire. Years ago.

JACK's face lights up and for once he looks like a human being, full of joy.

JACK: The Empire! Years ago! You saw that did you? (*Turning to gloat at WALLY and BETTY.*) Oh it was some show. It was the greatest…it was…the greatest thing that's ever happened to me.

BETTY: Up to a point.

Beat.

JACK: (*Turning and with slow fury.*) Don't you fucking… Don't you fucking dare!!! How *dare* you?

BETTY: Today of all days?

JACK: Aye, today of…

JACK is suddenly stunned. His face drops. He is staring at BETTY as if he's seen a ghost.

She nods.

JACK is horrified by something.

JACK: (*Barely above a whisper.*) Fuck….

BETTY stands and goes to exit. She stops and turns.

BETTY: Lorna? Can you tell my fortune?

LORNA is suspicious but nods anyway.

They exit.

CHARLIE: You were picking kids out of the audience?

JACK: (*Not listening.*) Kids…aye… The Empire.

CONNOR: I remember that act. The aunt and uncle stuff. Swell act. You and Betty.

JACK: She didnae do the Empire. I was only on one night.

CHARLIE: It was just you.

JACK: Aye. It was just me.

WALLY: (*Diverting from the strange atmosphere.*) You were saying you were wanting to tell us the truth about something?

CHARLIE: Well…em…I don't know what you've heard but… (*Quick glance at JACK who's miles away.*) I'm a talent scout from America. I'm scouting. For talent. (*To JACK.*) I'm the one picking on folk now. That's what scouts do. I thought it best that you all know. Know who I am.

CHARLIE has immediately had second thoughts. He and JACK seem to have identical expressions. Deep, deep regret.

WALLY: Well! This is a surprise eh lads?

CONNOR manages a little smile. Nobody looks happy about this except WALLY.

A bell rings and HARVEY appears.

HARVEY: That's it. Thirty minutes till Enter The Villagers. Clear the stage. Thirty minutes.

WALLY, CONNOR and JACK exit. They all have other things on their mind.

CHARLIE is left frozen.

CHARLIE: What have I done?

HARVEY: I don't know chap, what have you done?

CHARLIE: I'm pretending to be someone else.

HARVEY: Well you're in the right place.

CHARLIE: But what happens next?

HARVEY: (*Shrugs.*) The spice of life. (*Shouts up to the back of the theatre.*) Curtain! House Lights!

As the curtain closes and the house lights return we can hear EDWARD singing offstage.

EDWARD: (*Off.*) Tho' you're tired and weary still journey on, till you come to your happy abode,
Where all you love you've been dreaming of will be there...
At the end of the road.

End of Act One.

ACT TWO

Scene 1

CHARLIE is on the phone backstage.

HARVEY: (*Off.*) Thirty minutes!

CHARLIE: I realise that Arthur it's just that…no I didn't know that was what they cost. That's really quite…for napkins? Are you crying? Are you crying because of the wedding or because of the napkins? Right. Well I'm sure you'll… No it's just that things have taken a funny turn here and… (*Brightening.*) Did he? That was nice of him. Good old Hendry. (*Face drops.*) Did he? He read out my letter. What… Were they? Well it's good to have a laugh isn't it? No…I'm…flattered. Em…just not the sort of thing you would picture coming up in a speech at someone's wedding…No it's nothing. Just wanted to wish Fiona all my…best wishes. Oh no everything's fine here. It's all going according to plan.

HARVEY: (*Off.*) Thirty minutes till Enter The Villagers!

Arthur has hung up. CHARLIE still holds the phone. He doesn't want to go back to work. Just when he thinks things can't get worse he sees JACK. JACK has his hands in his pockets and is looking a bit hang-dog. He's there to see CHARLIE though and is determined to get what he wants even though he feels terrible.

JACK: Alright?

CHARLIE: (*Hanging up the phone.*) No. Not at all.

JACK: You should've told whoever it was to get to fuck. That's what I'd've done.

CHARLIE: You don't know Arthur.

JACK: Doesnae matter who it is, 'get to fuck!' It's the only language they understand.

CHARLIE: You don't know me either. I can't do that. I can't just…stand up for myself. It's pathetic. I just do whatever it is people want me to do. To please them. But it never works.

JACK: I know what you mean, I'm forever fucking pleasing people and are they fucking thankful? Are they fuck.

CHARLIE's not pleased. Not only does he have job worries he's remembered about JACK being his tormentor back at the Empire. Unhappy pause. Beat.

Here, this'll cheer you up. This is a stitch. I'll ask what your name is and you ask me, 'What's yours?', right?

CHARLIE: What?

JACK: (*His act voice.*) What's your name?

CHARLIE: Charles Buchanan.

JACK indicates he needs more to go on.

Charles Anthony Buchanan.

JACK: No. You say to me 'what's yours'.

CHARLIE: What's your name?

JACK: (*Happily.*) A large whiskey plea…(*Snap back.*) no! You say 'What's yours?'

CHARLIE: I've told you mine. I only have three names.

JACK: I don't care how many fucking names you've got, you just say 'What's yours?'

CHARLIE: I don't…

JACK: (*Furious.*) Just fucking say what's fucking yours!!! Fucking say the words!! What's yours!

CHARLIE: I don't know what's happening.

JACK: Just fucking repeat after fucking me… What's….

CHARLIE: (*Slowly.*) What's…

JACK: Fucking….

CHARLIE: Fucking…

JACK: Yours.

CHARLIE: Yours.

JACK: A large whiskey please! Ha ha ha ha. (*The laugh runs out of steam pretty quickly.*) Tch.

A big pause for wincing and regrets. It bombed.

CHARLIE: What is yours?

JACK: Jack Salt! Jack fucking Salt. Jesus wept.

CHARLIE: And you're the comedian?

JACK: Don't sound too fucking surprised.

CHARLIE: I remember you.

JACK: (*A bit brighter.*) Aye from my night at the Empire. That was some show eh? They were rolling in the aisles eh?

CHARLIE: Do you remember all your shows?

JACK: I remember that one. (*Down again.*) Every fucking detail of that day.

CHARLIE: Do you?

JACK: I'll never forget it.

CHARLIE: (*Nervous.*) So…so…so…are you sorry?

JACK: Am I sorry?

CHARLIE: Aye.

Big pause as JACK pulls himself up.

JACK: What are you getting at ya wee fucker? What do you know about that day? What the fuck do you know about anything? What's she said to you? What has she fucking said to you?

CHARLIE: Who?

JACK: Betty! She knows I want this, I need this! But she'll never forgive me for going to the Empire that night. That was my chance! I couldnae just no go, cos...cos *that* had happened. It wasnae my fucking fault. So don't ask me if I'm sorry. Aye I'm sorry. Sorry that she's filled your head with poison just tae stop my one chance of getting out of here alive. She's out the act son. Forever. And I'm so fucking sorry. But I'm good. I can be good again. I fucking know I can. You've just got to see me on a good night. (*Getting a bit frantic.*) You've got to see me, up close, see how I work, bouncing off people, bits of business flying off the top of my head, that's what you should see. I can do it. But I need someone, anyone, a stooge, someone I can use. But she's...but it's all...it's all...you should see...you should...you should... (*A light bulb.*) You should go on wi me instead of her! Aye, that's it. (*A threat.*) Anyone could do it. Aye that's it! Is that what you're wearing?

CHARLIE: Eh?

JACK: I've got comedy trousers if you would prefer them.

CHARLIE: Why would I...?

JACK: Gets an easy laugh on your entrance.

CHARLIE: What entrance? What are you talking about?

JACK: What do you fucking think? You're coming on with me instead of Betty.

CHARLIE: On stage!

JACK: You'll just be feeding me it'll be a piece of piss.

CHARLIE: Oh no. Oh no, no, no. I'm not going on stage. (*Even saying the word makes him feel sick.*) On stage. No. I can't. I can't.

JACK: How?

CHARLIE: I'll faint. Or die.

JACK: You'll no die. Me an her used to do an act where we picked wee idiots out the audience and made up gags about them. And don't listen to her. I could always think on my feet and get a laugh wi any fucking arsepiece standing beside me. And there needs to be someone cos that's the act. So it's you. Then you'll see how good I am for the pictures. Then you'll see. I need this son. I need this. I need this. I need this. (*Very close to literally begging.*) I fucking need this.

Something's clicked in CHARLIE.

HARVEY: (*Off.*) Fifteen minutes!

CHARLIE: I'll do it.

Scene 2

We are somewhere backstage. LORNA's room. Now maybe this isn't a dressing room, maybe it's just a nook that she hides in, but it's definitely her place. There are silks on the walls and candles and a few photographs. This is a place no-one has been in before. She sits at a table and is dealing Tarot cards or something similar. She is not alone. BETTY is with her. BETTY is drinking from a bottle of whiskey as she examines the room around her, gingerly touching the silks and peering at the photographs. She sees something she recognises.

HARVEY: (*Further off.*) Thirty minutes!

BETTY: (*About the photo*) Ah! Jimmy King. Where is this?

Looks like a seaside place? Girvan or somewhere.
Jimmy was some guy. Were you with his troupe long?
He's dead I think. Is he dead? I used to keep all this
stuff. All our bills and posters and cuttings. I got rid
of them. You've made this place nice. Silk? Nice. Ha!
Here's a picture of you standing outside the old Metropole. Who took this I wonder? You look happy. I played
the Metropole when I was sixteen. I was in the Simpson
Girls. A high-kicker. The Tartan Tillers. Those were
my wild days. (*Looking back at the picture*) Oh you're not
wearing your whatdoyoucallit – your dress. Your foreign
clothes. I've never seen you in normal clothes. You look
happy. Do you not get lonely down here? Mind you I
suppose it's peace and quiet for you eh? You can get up
to anything down here eh? No-one will ever catch you. I
wish I had went to a fortune teller back then. I could've
saved myself a liver. And a heart. But I never. I didn't
think I needed to. But you don't when you're young
do you? You're young. You're so young, compared to
me. You never speak when you're offstage. Not a word.
But I remember you speaking, when you first came
here, I remember you singing. To be honest I'm only
here to hear you speak. I'm only joking. Mind you, I
think I know what my fortune is. If I have the strength.
(*She takes a big drink*) Was it that night that stopped you
speaking? You used to sing and wear normal clothes
and everything I think. It was a horrible thing. He was
a bastard. I don't care how big a star he is in England,
he was a bastard to do that to you. Bastards all. I wanted
to say something, but I never. We all have our…we all
have our troubles. It's the spice of life isn't it? But the
show must go on.

HARVEY: (*Off.*) Thirty minutes till Enter The Villagers!

LORNA deals a card to BETTY.

BETTY takes a drink, not really paying attention.

BETTY: Why does the show have to go on? Today of all days. You probably think you know all about me and Jack. You've probably talked about us. Down here where no-one can hear you. But you don't know anything about us. It wasn't always horrible. But what could I do? The show must…today is my daughter's anniversary. I don't celebrate it. I'll celebrate her birthday but not this. I followed him to the theatre. Jack. On the very day it happened he went on stage. He said it was too big a chance to miss. The Glasgow Empire. Big time. He went on the very day our daughter died. Why I followed him I don't know, but I did. Maybe I thought I could steal some of his strength. But it wasn't strength that made him go on Lorna. I watched him from backstage.

BETTY looks to centre stage. JACK is there, but it's the giant from before. He has his back to the audience and is silhouetted by the cinema screen which shows a flickering image of a large audience laughing. The giant JACK is doing his act. We see CHARLIE joining him onstage, again silhouetted and with his back to us. We can't hear them as they do the scene from before.

I watched him pick a wee boy out of the audience. Then I worked it out. He knew. He knew that Rose wasn't his. I don't know how he knew but he did. And he didn't love her. My daughter who had died that day. And he didn't love me. His wife weeping in the wings.

BETTY takes a drink and the lights and screen fade on JACK and CHARLIE. She turns to LORNA with a sharper look in her eye.

You didn't know that did you? Down here where no-one can hear you. You don't know everything about us even though you think you do. (*Screaming.*) You don't know how I feel! (*Tiny.*) If you did, you wouldn't do it. You just wouldn't.

BETTY is now standing very close to LORNA.

LORNA's worried.

Don't ask me how I know. I just do. Does he love you? Does he? That's all I need to know. Maybe you're wondering what the big deal is eh? After all, he doesn't love me and we fight all the time and he's a pig nine times out of ten. But I need him. I need his coldness and his arrogance and his...detachment. I need it! But now it's all lost. I'm finished. All because a wee black lassie comes along. What did you do? How did you trap him? Lead him on did you? All shy and quiet down here where no-one can hear you? Yes. I'll bet that's what you did to whatshisname, the big star from England. Yes, he was a headliner too. Oh it all makes sense. You go after the top of the bill. Snare them and hope they'll drag you up with them. But maybe whatshisname didn't fall for it? Maybe that time he saw you for what you are? A whore wog. Maybe you said you were going to black-mail him and that's why he attacked you? Maybe that's what a whore wog needs? Eh? Maybe you wanted it? You wanted him on you!

BETTY hits LORNA violently in the face and grabs her, hitting her repeatedly. BETTY only stops when LORNA screams. It's the howl of a beaten animal suddenly biting back. All the composure and distance she has maintained throughout BETTY's speech disappear instantly. The fury of the scream pushes BETTY away.

LORNA: YOU'RE NOT ALLOWED TO TOUCH ME!!! No-one is to touch me! I don't want people to touch me.

LORNA curls into a ball.

BETTY feels terrible. She sits and drinks.

HARVEY: (*Off.*) Fifteen minutes!

BETTY: I didn't mean that.

LORNA: I don't want anyone to touch me. In any way! Anyone.

BETTY: Okay hen.

There's a pause as LORNA calms down. They don't look at each other. But when LORNA finally looks at BETTY it's her time to feel guilty.

LORNA: It's not a love affair.

BETTY: (*Lightly.*) Isn't it?

LORNA: No. He…he was the one who found me.

BETTY looks up.

It was Jack who found me. He heard me screaming and he came down. He was the one who pulled the man off of me. He was the one who hit the man and threw him out.

BETTY: Jack did?

LORNA: Yes. Jack did. Then he came back and made sure I was alright.

BETTY: Did he?

LORNA: But I wasn't alright. And he'd *seen* me, he'd seen me…at my worst. But he kept coming back.

BETTY: Oh I see.

LORNA: No! It's not that. I promise. I couldn't.

BETTY: So what do you do down here eh? Where no-one can hear you?

Pause.

LORNA: We…pretend.

BETTY: Eh?

LORNA: We pretend.

BETTY: Pretend what?

LORNA: We pretend that I'm his daughter and he's my father.

BETTY: Eh?

LORNA: We pretend that we're a family. We call it The Game.

This situation is too incredible for BETTY. She tries to imagine JACK playing that type of game. She can't. And yet there's something about it that rings true.

BETTY: What…what is it you do in the game?

LORNA: It's like an act. We have lines to say.

BETTY: But how…?

LORNA: It was the feelings that came first. He felt like my father. Then he just started talking and it became a habit. I'm sorry.

BETTY: And what does he say? What does he tell you?

LORNA: He calls me Rose.

Reaction from BETTY.

BETTY: Does he?

LORNA: He says it wasn't his fault. He keeps saying sorry.

BETTY: It wasnae his fault. It was mine.

LORNA: He says that too.

BETTY: (*Devastated.*) Aye. Oh well. I hope you'll both be happy.

There's a pause. Then BETTY throws the cards into the air. They catch the light as they scatter. LORNA catches one of them. Another silence.

LORNA: I'll never be happy. Do you know what a pariah is? In India it means someone with no caste. You have no standing. You don't count because there was something filthy about your birth. But it used to mean 'a drummer', because drummers didn't get to take part in the processions. They were seen as vulgar entertainers, too crude for high religious celebrations. Here it means someone who is a reject, an outsider, a despised and loathed foreigner. I am all of these things. I am a pariah. So I will never be happy.

BETTY: Looks at us both eh?

LORNA: My father was a soldier.

BETTY looks at LORNA. This wee announcement came a little out of the blue and she doesn't really know what to do about it.

BETTY: (*Smiles through tears*) That's nice.

LORNA looks like she's holding back a big outburst and is moving strangely.

LORNA: The thing about pariah's – all pariahs – is that they are fortune tellers in some sort of way. And the only real way to tell a fortune, is for something to die. Sometimes chickens or oxen are slaughtered and their guts deciphered, sometimes it's snakes or sometimes even people. Over the years people have become squeamish about it. It's all hoodoo. Left to acts like me on the stage. Now it's cards and tea and palm readings. But if you really want to know what's going to happen, something has to die.

BETTY: (*Far away.*) Yeah. I know. What does my card say?

LORNA looks at the card in her hand which she plucked out the sky.

HARVEY: (*Off.*) Ten Minutes!

LORNA: It says that you're stronger than you think you are.

BETTY: (*Flatly.*) Strong enough to tell my own future. Uncanny.

BETTY gets up to leave. As she gets to the door:

BETTY: Can I...pretend? Can I pretend to be your mother?

The look in LORNA's face is the answer.

BETTY: No. Daft really. I'm sorry though. I want you to know that I'm sorry.

BETTY exits.

Scene 3

BETTY is leaving LORNA's room, upset and carrying her whisky bottle. She passes CONNOR, who is now dressed in a kilt. HARVEY zooms past.

HARVEY: Ten minutes!

Exit HARVEY.

CONNOR: Have a good one Betty. Betty? Are you alright, hen?

BETTY: Happy for tabs.

CONNOR: Do you want to have a wee chinwag? We've got time.

BETTY: Do we?

WALLY appears.

WALLY: Ten minutes. Right Connor, let's sort you out for tonight.

CONNOR: In a minute Wallace old son. (*To BETTY.*) Are you sure you're...

HARVEY is heard, or even seen somewhere.

HARVEY: (*Off.*) Enter the Villagers! Ten minutes.

WALLY: Connor now!!

A pause for CONNOR to count to ten. He decides to shrug it off and rolls his eyes for BETTY's benefit. He disappears with WALLY.

BETTY: Thank you.

There's a moment with BETTY alone, before ED-WARD appears. Maybe he's been there all along. He's busy taking something apart and moving key pieces of equipment. He doesn't look round at BETTY but senses she's there.

EDWARD: I'm dismantling the apparatus! I'm opening the cages and letting all the souls go before they are taken prisoner by machines and... (*Turns and sees that it's BETTY. Drops the act completely. He becomes calm.*) Oh it's you.

BETTY: Yeah it's me, Eddie. You can drop it.

EDWARD: Drop what?

BETTY: The drama. I've had my fill.

EDWARD: (*Smiling.*) You should've seen me early on. It was just like the old days. Barking outside the waxworks on Sauchihall street 'Beware! Beware!' You would've been proud of me.

BETTY: Let me guess (*Doing impression.*) 'There's laughter in the walls! Human beings and other human beings!'

EDWARD: (*Going along with the teasing.*) No. Well... And anyway I seem to remember that little speech going

down fairly well with a certain young dancer not too
long ago.

BETTY: Ha! Is that what you think it was? Your eccentric
theatrical bit? No. That wasn't it.

EDWARD: What was it then? The fiddle playing? The clog
dancing?

BETTY:You were a political romantic. A deadly combina-
tion. But that was a long time ago. I'm not that young
dancer and you gave all your politics and romance
away years ago.

EDWARD: I'm sure you can still dance if asked by an old
romantic.

*EDWARD takes the bottle out of her hand, takes a swig,
puts it on the floor and pulls BETTY in a gentle dance.
There might be music. BETTY laughs at the gesture but
goes along with it.*

BETTY: So who was your act in aid of? Some starry eyed
hopeful?

EDWARD: No. This was serious. This was do or die. I was
trying to scare someone away.

BETTY: Who?

EDWARD: The wee Irish chap.

BETTY: God. He's scared enough as it is. Why? Do you
honestly think he'll see something here he wants?

EDWARD: He already has.

BETTY: Has he? (*Thinking it's JACK and sadly.*) So it is
over?

EDWARD: No no no. I'll sort it. I've organized something
special for tonight. Harry's coming!

He breaks off from the dancing.

Harry Lauder, the great man himself is coming here.

BETTY: No he's not.

EDWARD: He is! I pulled some strings and scratched some backs. Harry'll come and Buchanan and his moving pictures will see the error of their ways and forget the whole thing…

He's getting excited and just a bit unhinged.

BETTY: Edward…

EDWARD: I have it here. (*Reading the letter*) 'Mr Lauder understands and would love to be of some aid.' I told him the deadline and he's never late. The utmost professional. Dance with me again Elizabeth. I can't remember the last time we danced.

BETTY: Eleven years to the day.

EDWARD: (*Thinks she's joking.*) Ha ha. A long time.

BETTY: Eleven years to the day. Edward how are you feeling? Have you had any more…turns?

EDWARD: Turns? I remember when I used to be a turn, now I have them.

BETTY: Can I see Harry Lauder's letter?

EDWARD: Why?

BETTY: I just…

EDWARD: You don't believe me? You want to prove that I'm living in a delusion? That I'm putting on an act to avoid my responsibility. Avoiding reality. Harry Lauder will come don't worry. (*Looking at the letter with doubt for the first time.*) I'll be waiting for him. I'll be… I'll be… (*Reads the letter.*)…waiting for him.

EDWARD realises that he's misunderstood the letter. He rips it up. He has to sit down. He puts his head in his hands. BETTY sits beside him. They pass the bottle between them.

It's the illness. It takes everything from you bit by bit. First it was my touch, then my eyes and now my mind. I can't believe what's happened. It's like I'm a child. Who'd've thought I'd actually go mad eh?

BETTY: You're not mad Edward. You're ill. And desperate. It's normal.

EDWARD: No. It's not normal. After all my pretending, it's came true. There's irony in there somewhere. I can no longer tell the difference between my act and my real life. But it's the illness. The building has it too did you know that? (*Ashamed.*) I see things too.

BETTY: (*Dreading what's coming.*) Do you?

EDWARD: I do. I see her. I see her here. It's Rose. Sometimes it's like I've let her out. Like the laughter in the walls, do you know what I mean? All my talk has came true and the souls are here. She's here. I don't know what she wants.

BETTY: (*Sad.*) She wants her mum. (*Getting angry.*) She doesn't want you. You were nothing to her. For all your talk of the future and of running away, you did nothing. Nothing. You were nothing to her. And you were nothing to me! And that makes it so much worse. Can you understand that? That I was upstairs with a man who meant nothing to me while my daughter…while she… And I'm lying on a dressing room couch with a man who meant nothing. I can't be forgiven for that. So don't you dare say that you see her! Because you don't deserve to see her! Why can't I see her? I want to see her so much.

EDWARD: We can run away now. We can leave this place to Buchanan and the cinema people. I can make it up to you. I'll get well. I'll be sane and responsible and I'll never see her again. I can be like I used to be.

BETTY: The cinema people?

EDWARD: The wee fella. They've bought this place and it's going to be a cinema. I didn't tell you…because… because…it slipped through my fingers. So we can go and we'll leave nothing behind.

BETTY: (*Gives a strange laugh on the landing of the final straw.*) We'll leave nothing behind. I've only ever wanted a connection. A human connection. And I've never found it. Except on stage. It was my favourite place.

BETTY gets up. ROSE appears. This time it's BETTY who sees her. She smiles.

She wants her mum.
ROSE exits and BETTY follows.

EDWARD: (*Shouting off.*) I'm sorry. I'll fight it. I can save it. With or without Harry Lauder. (*Looks at his hands.*) Someone's got to fight against the tide. Make it like it was, away from all the…new. I'll protect your stage Betty. I promise. It's my favourite place too.

EDWARD goes to exit but stops. He comes back, picks up the ripped letter and reads it. He can't let go of the idea completely.

Scene 4

This scene takes place at the same time as the last one. This time we're in a small, quick change room, with a little mirror and a prop table and some bizarre costumes hanging on a rack. There is a door which can lock. WALLY is in the room, peering out the door. WALLY is extremely wound up by nerves. CONNOR seems to have his mind on something else.

HARVEY: (*Off.*) Enter the villagers! Ten minutes!

WALLY: Connor now!!

Enter CONNOR.

CONNOR: There's something wrong with poor old Betty. Does she seem a bit off to you?

WALLY: Ach, she's always off, you'd be off too if you were stuck with Jack. Listen, see tonight...

CONNOR: It's amazing she's stuck with him.

WALLY: Yeah, see tonight...

CONNOR: It's amazing why some people stick together.

WALLY: Connor shut up! This is important. It's more than important it's...it's...everything.

CONNOR: Okay, calm down mate. What's wrong?

WALLY: Don't tell me to calm down. Are you doing the new stuff tonight? The new stuff I gave you yesterday?

CONNOR produces some scraps of paper from his sporran.

CONNOR: Yes...em...it's very good, as usual. But it does seem rather...

WALLY: (*Grabbing the papers and ripping them up.*) Forget it. You're doing the old stuff. You're clearer on that. It needs to be clear and sharp tonight. No mistakes. And none of your bloody work songs. Just the heather and lassies pish. I don't need any controversy.

CONNOR: Oh I see. For the film chap. Wally...?

WALLY: And don't give us any of that 'working man suffers' nonsense. We both know where you come from. I was the first working class person you'd ever met and I was only there cos my aunt did your kitchen.

CONNOR: Wally, this business with the man from the film place...

WALLY: Film place? RKO! That's America, that's money, that's getting out of this....this slide. How you feeling? Strong? How's the voice? Do you need anything?

CONNOR: No, fine. Wally....

WALLY: (*Getting excited and unused to the feeling.*) God! This is it Connor. I can feel it. I knew I was right. I knew it. It's so close. I'm nervous. Can you believe that? I can't remember the last time I was nervous.

CONNOR drops what he wanted to tell WALLY for the moment. He's happy to see WALLY happy.

CONNOR: I do. Aberdeen. Remember that? Aberdeen?

WALLY laughs.

You were so nervous you were sick in a tuba. I had to go on myself.

WALLY: That wasn't stage fright though, that was cos Irene Hunter's dad had brought along a gang of apes and they were all sitting in the front row ready to pelt me with rivets. Lying cow. I was in fear for my life. And I wasn't sick in a tuba. It was a euphonium.

They both laugh.

CONNOR: That was the first time I performed alone. I kept looking over to the wings to make sure you were still there. I was nervous then too. (*The laughter's running out.*) Actually, that was the night you said you wanted to split up the act. You'd had the idea for your new look and everything. Dr Walford Chipo! You said you felt you'd have a better chance on your own. Do you remember that?

WALLY: (*Sadly.*) Yeah.

HARVEY: (*Off.*) Five minutes!

CONNOR: Wally? Why don't we put the old act together? Just for tonight. It would be a dream come true. We were good Wally. Do you want to? Wally?

WALLY: Connor…I can't believe you're dragging up all these bloody…ghosts. The old act's dead. It's dead. My act's refined, the RKO guy said he was here to *specifically* see me. But he trusts my opinion and I went out of my way for you Connor.

CONNOR: I know.

WALLY: I bent over backwards to get him to look at you. And I know you think I'm a charity case. Poor wee Wallace the urchin, taken in from the cold by the wonderful McNair family, forever to be pitied. I'm not a sidekick anymore. I'm your manager and if I decide to pass on RKO's offer for my act it'll be because I'm willing to stand to one side to get you to the top.

CONNOR: Wally? What if I don't want to get to the top?

WALLY: I beg your pardon?

CONNOR: I said…

WALLY: Oh I heard you. And I heard you last month when you said it then. And I heard you two years ago when it first came up. And so on and so on. And what happens every time we have the 'I'm leaving the show' chat?

CONNOR: Nothing.

WALLY: Correct. Because you always change your mind. You're just scared of success. You say you want out of show business and that you'd be happy in a real job just keeping yourself to yourself. But you don't and you won't. You never leave. Because you know you'd be miserable.

CONNOR: I know. (*A change.*) You could come too.

WALLY: Ha!

CONNOR: We used to say that we'd run a wee café together? Remember that? I've got money. We can go tonight. This place is a coffin.

WALLY: Connor…I…I can't believe…that stuff is a million years old! Just adolescent…I mean why would you bring that up? Are you trying to humiliate me?

CONNOR: No! We could be happy. That's all.

WALLY: Happy? I'll give you happy. Hollywood is happy. Fame is happy. Money is happy. That's happiness.

CONNOR: So being with me wouldn't…

WALLY: Being with you? Why does everything always come back to you? What about me? When do I get a shot eh? Why am I still getting thrown your scraps? When's that going to change? I'm sorry Connor. It's just that I believe in you. I know you can do this. In fact I believe in you so much that if Buchanan doesn't want you for RKO…then…then we'll do it your way. (*Laughing.*) We'll run a café.

CONNOR: (*Coldly.*) I don't believe you.

WALLY: (*Still laughing.*) Yes you do. You believe everything I tell you.

CONNOR: Please don't laugh at me.

WALLY: (*Laughing.*) You're so gullible sometimes…

CONNOR: Oh shut up.

WALLY: Some of the things…

CONNOR: I don't believe any of it. It's an act.

WALLY: Ha ha… 'A chimp took it I swear…'

CONNOR: Wally shut up.

WALLY: Ooooh! Temper temp…

CONNOR: SHUT UP! (*He does*) He's not from RKO.

WALLY: What?

CONNOR: He's not from RKO.

WALLY: What's that meant to mean?

CONNOR: It means he's not from RKO. He's not from a film company at all. Christ any fool can see that.

WALLY: (*Pause*) Well I never thought I'd see the day. The worm has turned eh? I knew you were low but not this low. So what was the plan, put me off my act? Or was it so that you could wriggle out the contract and sign for him by yourself? Eh? Well I've got news for you, without me you're nothing. You're a joke. Everyone laughs at you, with your daft old songs and your fucking…kilt. And *all* the other stuff. Aye they laugh about that too. I'm the one sticking up for you and now this. You're a sad old joke. You're a relic. The guy's from RKO alright because I wrote to him asking him to come. It's all down to me.

CONNOR: The man you wrote to from RKO came from London. He was English, not Irish. He was old, not young. It was me he wanted, not you. He came last month, not today. And I said no.

Big pause for WALLY to take this in.

WALLY: Naw. That's a lie.

CONNOR: It's not. But I said no. For you. He didn't want

you so I turned him down. For some reason I can't leave you behind. I love you. I still love you Wallace.

WALLY: (*Tiny.*) That's a fucking lie.

CONNOR: I…I love you I'm saying.

WALLY turns slowly and looks at CONNOR coldly.

WALLY: You love me?

CONNOR: Always. You know that.

WALLY: Kiss me then.

CONNOR: Eh?

WALLY: Kiss me.

CONNOR: But you said…

WALLY: I've changed my mind. Come on Connor, it's what you've wanted all these years. Do something for yourself for a change. You're right. We can leave. Run away from the lights and be happy. You were right, I was wrong. It's time to be honest.

CONNOR leans down to kiss WALLY. He's shaking with nerves. Just as their lips are about to touch, WALLY spits in CONNOR's face. It's as vicious as a punch to CONNOR and sends him to the floor in shock, hands to his face. WALLY looks at him in disgust.

It's sad.

CONNOR: It is!

WALLY: I've got a new contract for you. A verbal contract. Or you could think of it as new lines for the old act. It goes like this; you'll go back to RKO cap in hand and *beg* to sign a contract. You'll say you made an incredible mistake. But you'll be under my management. I make all the decisions. *All* the decisions! Or I tell. I'll tell everyone what you are. And I'm not just talking about show folk. I'm talking about good old Mr and Mrs McNair and the rest of my wonderful adopted family. We'll see how much Christian charity they have in their hearts then. We'll see how you like it to be pitied.

CONNOR: I thought we were at least friends.

WALLY: It's amazing why some people stick together.

We hear HARVEY shout from off louder than his other calls.

HARVEY: Enter the villagers!!!!

WALLY: Beginners. Clean yourself up. You never know who might be watching.

They get ready for the show.

Scene 5

HARVEY: Maybe you know the feeling? The moment before the curtain pulls back and there's music to be faced. It's not a frantic kind of fear. It's a low, rumbling, calm fear which comes when you have no way out. You have to go on, if only for the other performers, so why kick and scream? Maybe you know that feeling. It's a line I've never crossed. I'm high up in the dark, or black in the shadows, skipping from any sliver of light in case I'm seen and the show is spoiled. I stay quiet. I've never felt the heat of the lights or spoken in that unnatural air. I've never crossed over. Never performed. Even now, in my favourite place, I'll never cross over. Tomorrow won't come for me. I'm here to do my job. To make sure the show goes over with no hitches. And I do it night after night, forever and ever. Maybe it's because I don't get it right? I try! I try every time but…I'm not an Empire boy. Not yet. Maybe it *is* my fault? Maybe, deep down I want to be seen? Maybe I'm fed up with the shadows and tip-toes? Maybe that's why I never quite make it? I always miss. Always. Maybe you know the feeling? (*Shouts the announcement.*) Enter The Villagers! (*HARVEY disappears and the curtain drops. We hear the band tuning up and the ghostly echo of HARVEY's cueing rings round the building, overlapping.*) Stand by MD. Dots and bows up. (*The tuning up stops.*) House clearance, limes primed. Standby Tommy go Tommy standby Jimmy go Jimmy standby Andy go Andy standby Billy go Billy standby Richard go Richard. Stand by MD go MD. (*There's a sudden silence as the MD cues the band. The silence has apparently caught JACK by surprise.*)

JACK: (*Off.*) If he's not from fucking RKO where the fuck is he fucking from?

HARVEY: (*Off.*) Ssssssh!!!!!

JACK: (*Off and in a tiny whisper.*) Fuck off.

Cueing chord from the band.

Scene 6

And here is the show. Curtain swoops and fanfare. The music starts and seems to be a jaunty '20s style vamp. But like all of the following section it is somehow warped, as if at the heart of it, something's wrong. It's like a memory of a dream; what's here is the essence of the performance if not the details. What we have now are snaps shots of the acts without sound. This can be as stylised as required, slow or quick, but each should be alone in light when mentioned and the audience should know that these parts are not to be seen as real. This is a montage. The music continues throughout snapping back to the reality of the opening number which is a 'meet the gang' type thing. JACK, WALLY, CONNOR and LORNA enter in a line with a gap where BETTY should be. They are trying their best to be troopers, but they all carry the baggage from their previous duologues. They sing.

ALL: It's Showtime! It's Showtime!
    Time to hide all your frowns away.
    It's Showtime! It's Showtime!
    Save your worries for another day.
    It's Showtime! It's Showtime!

MEN: It's sure a swell time to sing and dance.

ALL: It's Showtime! It's Showtime!

WOMEN: C'mon gals let's take a chance.

CONNOR: There is going to be some laughs and gags,
    So come along with us.
    There's going to be some singing
    And a hoodoo sorceress.

Music stops.

LORNA: (*Scowling.*) I foresee japes and merriment.

Music change. We flash forward/backward into a glimpse of LORNA's act. She is foreseeing the future and pulling huge faces as she writhes about, all her predictions are pessimistic and doom-laden. Suddenly we snap back to the reality of the opening number.

ALL: It's Showtime! It's Showtime!
    Surprises and fun galore.
    It's Showtime! It's Showtime!
    You'll be shouting out for more.

CONNOR: Pretty gals and handsome fellas
    Some faces you're sure to know

WALLY: I'm Dr Walford Chipo!

We see WALLY's act on one side of the stage. This can be as mad as you wish. WALLY's act is a mixture of every novelty act he's ever seen. Only he's not very good.

He juggles, balances, does 'electric magic' and plays the trick fiddle. He is in silence. On the other side of the stage CONNOR sings unaccompanied 'Ae Fond Kiss'.

CONNOR: Ae fond kiss, and then we sever
As fareweel, and then forever,
Deep in heart-wrung tears I'll pledge thee,
Warring sighs and groans I'll wage thee.
Who shall say that fortune grieves him
While the star of hope she leaves him?
Me, nae cheerfu' twinkle lights me,
Dark despair around benights me.

There is a moment when EDWARD's voice can be heard shadowing the last two lines from somewhere in the theatre. This snaps back to the reality of the opening song.

ALL: It's Showtime! It's Showtime!
We got stars and skits and laughter
It's Showtime! It's Showtime!
We got happy ever after.

JACK: Yer huving me on
Keep your eye on the baw,
I'm bound to get a thrill.
When I'm outta here, dump the old dear,
And get sweet with the chorus girl.

(*Speaks.*) I'm joking of course Ladies and Gentlemen. It's my utmost pleasure to introduce…

They have a beat to look at each other in panic. Obviously JACK's forgotten.

My lovely old dear, Betty Kemble…

He trails off into silence. The music starts again but has to stop as JACK winces, realises that she's not there. He freezes as we can hear BETTY playing the accordion. There is the mixture of applause and laughter heard from the walls as JACK sadly remembers the heydays.

The accordion seems to be coming from high up. JACK snaps out of it and shrugs off his embarrassment like the pro he is. He indicates to the band they should continue. They do.

ALL: It's Showtime! It's Showtime!
And now with no more ado
It's Showtime! It's Showtime!
Let's bring….

The music slows, finale style.

The show…
To…

JACK: Keep yer eye on the baw!

ALL: YOU!!!

End of opening number. They scamper off.

Scene 7

After a bit of fill-in music JACK swaggers onstage to his theme tune. He's followed, after a bit of nasty encouragement, by CHARLIE. Whatever the opposite to swagger is, CHARLIE's doing it. JACK mugs and grins at the audience. CHARLIE is wearing a pair of comedy trousers. He feels like a man sentenced to death. He stares at the audience in frozen terror. JACK throws him over to BETTY's normal spot on stage, giving a look as if to say, 'I'm gonna get you for this.'

JACK: Yer huving me on! Keep yer eye on the baw!

Pause for what we imagine should be BETTY's line. Nothing from CHARLIE. He's dead.

What that's yer saying darling…eh…darling, why's my face tripping me? You can talk. You've got a face like a bulldog licking treacle off a thistle. You're so fat to get on your good side I have to go two streets doon and

74

turn left. (*Pause.*) Oh you. Oh you nothing.

There's a seed of panic in JACK here. He speeds up and gives the mummified CHARLIE the odd hate-filled glare.

Eh…ha ha…yer eh…keep yer eye on the baw! Oh aye, that's right, I'll tell you why my face is tripping me. I tried to buy a motor car, but I didnae have enough money. I said to the fellow, 'what's the cheapest vehicle you have in stock?' He says, 'The cheapest thing we have is this desirable little carriage here.' And he brings out a hoop and a stick. A hoop and a stick! A bargain at a bob. And low! And low ladies and gentlemen, did it go? Did it go this hoop and stick? It did. It did go. It went. And I went with it. I was as happy as a wee lamb. A wee lamb, happy as a clam. Away, away, away I went through the city, with my hoop and stick, a veritable blur! Through the city and away up into the country. Now it was about four o'clock and nearly my bedtime, so I stopped in a wee pub for a swift medicinal. I left my hoop and stick outside, next to the donkeys and wheelbarrows. It was quite close to Paisley this pub. Anyroads I had a swift half. Then a slightly slower half. Then a couple more halves that werenae going anywhere. So I stumble out feeling faint and confusable about three hours later…and lo! What's happened? Someone's nicked my hoop and stick! That's what happens when you set a joke near Paisley! 'Yer huving me on!' I says to myself. I fly back into the pub as graceful as a swallow, and say 'Thievery and villainy of the gravest order! Someone's away wi' my hoop and my stick!!!' The barman goes, 'Okay calm down my friend, have another drink'. 'Never mind that,' I say. 'How am I meant to get home?'

JACK turns smugly to CHARLIE and nods.

(*Stage whisper.*) Do your bit.

CHARLIE: What bit?

JACK: I don't know. Your bit. (*To audience.*) The old dear is going to do an impersonation. (*To CHARLIE.*) You're good at that aren't you? Pretending to be other people.

There are mumbles from the audience who know something's wrong. CHARLIE is doomed.

CHARLIE: Em…eh…em…what's yours?

JACK: What's…eh?

CHARLIE: A whisky. A double whisky. Sorry.

Again a long awkward silence. JACK turns.

JACK: Well this is swell. Make Jack look like a f… broomstick. Eh? This is all a good laugh for the old dear. Look at her there. What a sight. She's got a face like a bulldog licking… Making me look like a broomstick. Pretending to be someone to get my hopes up. Probably everyone's in on it eh? Only I'm not the one who looks like a broomstick am I ladies and gentlemen?

A heckle or two.

Oh is that right? What do yous know? I played the Empire. I'm a f… I'm a star. All you rubes can get back to Paisley. And take yer sisters with ye!

A couple of jeers and boos now.

You're lucky to have me here ya bunch of spear-chucking, soap-fearing, muck farmers!

Offstage we can see HARVEY twirling his lasso ready to get JACK off the stage. The audience are getting really nasty, shouting out heckles and throwing the occasional missile.

(*Desperate.*) What are you picking on me for? Look at

who I'm standing next to. Look at the face. Ha ha, what a sight. And…oh wait a minute. What's this? Squinty eyes! Everyone! Everyone! Look at the squinty eyes on this specimen! Have ye ever seen anything like it? One eye looking for ye the other eye looking by ye. Ha ha ha.

There are a couple of laughs, in amongst the unhappy audience.

(*Getting back into his stride.*) It's like two fried eggs on a sinking ship. I say keep yer eye on the baw and he says, 'Which one?'

CHARLIE has been boiling for a while now but this is where the lid comes flying off.

CHARLIE: (*Screaming.*) I do not have a squint! I don't have one. It's my eye brows. I have lopsided eyebrows. Easy as that!

JACK: They look squinty to me, Squinty Eyes.

CHARLIE: They're not!

JACK: Squinto!

CHARLIE: Well at least I'm not mean!

Pause.

JACK: Mean?

CHARLIE: Aye, mean! (*Turning to the audience.*) I tried to light a fire once and he nearly died, (*Doing a impersonation.*) 'Coal costs money Buchanan!' Aye, coal costs money, but he wasnae using coal, he was using horse dung he'd picked up off the road!

To everyone's surprise, not least CHARLIE's, this gets a laugh. He continues.

He's so mean when he wants to smoke he stands on the

railway bridge and breathes in.

Another laugh.

He's got a photograph of a farthing on his mantelpiece. He plays snooker three times a week with the guy who owns the snooker hall. In his will he's leaving the guy a snooker. He's so mean!

Big laughs. CHARLIE is well on a roll.

At his wedding they got a sketch artist in instead of a photographer. When his wife wants to go to the pictures, he cuts the cartoons out of the paper and wiggles them in front of her eyes. Poor woman thinks Rudolph Valentino looks like Hen Broon. He's so mean!

A big laugh and applause. The band takes this as a cue for the end of the act and strikes up a chord. JACK tries to stop them but the lights have changed and the screen is dropping for the first picture show to start. CHARLIE is victorious and strong now. JACK knows it. He stands helpless and defeated. A short news reel, silent of course, starts on the screen and they exit.

Scene 8

Somehow, we are behind the screen immediately following CHARLIE and JACK's exit. LORNA is there waiting to go on. CHARLIE is excited beyond measure. HARVEY is scuttling about at high speed. Everything is done in excited whispers. And excited doesn't begin to describe CHARLIE. JACK sits on the floor defeated.

CHARLIE: Laughs! There were laughs.

JACK: Aye.

CHARLIE: They were laughing. At me! Well not *at* me, but at me.

JACK: Aye.

CHARLIE: I feel like I'm an explosion. I feel exploded. I've never…It's like I'm sparkling inside. (*Loud.*) I want to shout out to the world!

HARVEY: Sssh!

CHARLIE: (*Whisper.*) I want to shout out to the world, 'I'm a comedian! I've finally done it!'. I'm a comedian.

JACK: (*Resigned.*) Good for you. You can have my costume box if you want it. You can take my act, for all it's worth.

CHARLIE: What do you mean?

JACK: I mean I'm finished. I've been finished for years. Since the night I bombed at the Empire.

CHARLIE: People laughed at the Empire.

JACK: No-one laughed.

CHARLIE: No-one laughed?

JACK: No-one laughed.

CHARLIE: (*For a second doubting everything he's known as true.*) But I remember it.

JACK: Memories are funny things.

They both think about this for a second, but it's CHARLIE who brushes it off.

CHARLIE: You should teach me! You should teach me to be a comic. I want to be like you.

JACK: Naw. You don't want to be like me son. I'm fucked. I'm out. But tell me this, was it her?

CHARLIE: Eh?

JACK: Was it Betty. Is this stuff about Hollywood and everything just to get me back? Because it worked. I'm finished now.

CHARLIE: Oh. Aye. I'd forgotten about that. Sorry. It was my fault. I kind of…em…made it up.

JACK: Did you?

CHARLIE: Aye.

JACK: Why?

CHARLIE: Because…

JACK looks so broken he can't say.

I don't know. But it wasn't Betty. I've never even met her.

JACK: I love her.

CHARLIE: I could be in your act. If you let me. And Betty too. You could teach me. I could say 'He's so mean!' like a catchphrase. Please.

JACK: Who are you really?

CHARLIE: I'm Charlie Buchanan. I work for the people who are buying over this place. The cinema people. There's sound tomorrow.

JACK: Is there? I need to speak to my wife.

CHARLIE: What about the rest of the show?

JACK: (*Pause.*) I don't care.

CHARLIE: Maybe Edward will let me go on! I'll ask. What'll I do though? Ha ha this is A-One! I feel like I'm a different person.

CHARLIE exits leaving LORNA and JACK looking at each other.

HARVEY enters looking up into the rigging as if he sees something that shouldn't be there. He exits during the following exchange. Maybe there's a film on the screen behind them, shown in reverse as they are standing behind it.

LORNA: What will you do?

JACK: Nothing.

LORNA: What about The Game?

JACK: We'll have to stop it. We should have stopped a while ago.

LORNA: Betty already knows.

JACK: Did you tell her?

LORNA: Yes.

JACK: Oh well. Fuck. I've never really known what it was all about.

LORNA: It was just a game.

JACK: I know. I've always been better at rehearsals than performances.

LORNA: Do you want to do it now? We could finish our game.

JACK: Eh?

LORNA: We could finish it. You could be saying goodbye to me, the daughter. And you could be saying that you'd miss me. You could be saying that even though I'd never see you, you'd never forget me. You could say that maybe one day you'd come back and take me away. No matter where I was, even if I was always travelling and using a different name, you'd still find me and take me away. You could say that and then that way I could always hope it'd happen. It'd keep me going. I'd have a future to look into.

JACK: You'll be alright.

LORNA: I won't though. I know I won't.

JACK: It's over now.

LORNA: Just say it! Say that you're my dad and you're coming back for me! Say it!

HARVEY: (*Off.*) Ssshhh!!

JACK: I was only pretending. I don't know how it all started but it's finished now.

LORNA: But I need the game.

There is a loud crash behind them and cries from the audience as a large part of the screen collapses. Everyone, except BETTY, appears to see what's happened.

Scene 9

EDWARD has happened, that's what. He has unhooked a side of the cinema screen and it has fallen to the stage dramatically. The film stops. Edward appears, still trying to dismantle the screen. The others, still with the exception of Betty are standing onstage. No-one seems to have the energy to stop him.

HARVEY: Oh chap. You've buggered my screen!

EDWARD: (*To the 1929 audience and angrier and realer than we've seen him so far.*) Go on! Leave! Your precious screen is dead. That's right leave.

HARVEY: There going.

EDWARD: They're going but they'll be back. This is their favourite place, a sacred place. They'll be back. So Mr Buchanan I couldn't scare you away, I couldn't talk you away and I couldn't dream you away. But I've hatched a plan. I've come to my senses…

HARVEY: Obviously.

EDWARD: I don't know why I didn't think of this before. If there's no screen there'll be no pictures. Simple really. Mind you some of the best acts were the simple ones. Go on. Get hold of your boss and tell him that he can't have us. The building is wrecked and the laughter has been let loose. Tell him his screen is no more. Mr Harvey, help me with the other side.

CHARLIE: I'll help you. I'm not going back to Western Electricals. Arthur can…can…get to fuck. He's so mean!

CHARLIE goes to help EDWARD. HARVEY doesn't move. He looks pre-occupied and scared.

EDWARD: Come on! We can do this ourselves. We don't need Lauder or fantasies or ghosts. People need this place as it is. It's got to stay exactly as it is!

HARVEY: It can't. It won't…

EDWARD: Mr Harvey, lasso this monstrosity to the ground.

HARVEY: No.

EDWARD: We've got to. I promised. We've got to fight.

HARVEY: (*Angry.*) Fight what? Nothing you can do will change this. Time moves on. The tides change. Some things will always get left behind. It's not right and it's not wrong. It's just the way it is.

EDWARD: No! We can resist it. We can fight. We have to.

HARVEY: But it makes no difference.

EDWARD: You don't know. You don't know what happens next? You can't see the future. No-one can.

HARVEY: *I* can. I know what happens next because it always happens. It happens over and over again…

HARVEY turns away and starts to unravel his lasso.

Over and over and over and over…

EDWARD: No, we can dam the tide, and pull the drawbridge. I'm seeing clearly now. We can keep right on till…

ROSE appears looking up.

JACK: Where is she Todd?

EDWARD: (*Miles away.*) Mmm…?

HARVEY: And over and over…

JACK: Where's my wife?

HARVEY: And over and over…

JACK: And don't lie to me any more. I need to see her.

EDWARD follows ROSE's gaze. As do we. We look up, slowly the darkness above the stage is illuminated. Then we can see her. High above them, standing on a precarious ledge is BETTY. She has a far away look in her eye and is getting ready to jump. She spreads her arms wide as if she were preparing to fly. There are some shouts from the players on the stage.

EDWARD: Elizabeth.

JACK: Betty. Betty hen! (*Almost a whisper.*) I'm sorry.

EDWARD: I'm sorry.

LORNA: I'm sorry.

CHARLIE: I'm sorry.

CONNOR: Betty darling! Don't do anything daft honey. Come down. We'll get through it. We'll stick together like we've always done. No-one's leaving anyone. Solidarity. (*Looks to WALLY.*) It's only variety. It's not important. It's something people do for fun. Oh, it's just so fucking…*trivial!*

BETTY smiles and nods. She agrees.

Lights change so that it's just HARVEY and BETTY in spotlights. HARVEY is slowly unravelling his lasso. He talks to the audience.

HARVEY: And so here it is. This is why I'm here I suppose. The same moment, again and again and again. In my favourite place. My favourite time. And I do it night after night, forever and ever. (*He's twirling the lasso like a trick cowboy now.*) It's strange what you remember. For instance I don't remember anyone else there except for me. In my mind, and therefore forever, it was an empty stage. But I remember the projector was on. It was the footage Charlie needed for his big opening. I remember thinking that they should be happy. If all this was about being remembered, about immortality, then they had it. They were on screen.

The stage is filled with projected footage of the acts from the show. We see the theatre full of smiling people, in period dress. Then we see each of the players doing their act, except in front of that period audience, including CHARLIE and JACK's bit. The footage is rough and fast but it has a genuine feel to it. It is, of course, silent. It projects over the entire stage, not just the screen.

Maybe it's always been my decision? That I should be stuck, here in this moment, over and over. Maybe I have enough hope that something could be different? That I could be an Empire Boy, away from the ghosts and the regret and the laughter in the walls. Just once. Maybe.

BETTY jumps into darkness and at the same instant HARVEY throws his lasso aimed straight for her. The spotlights on both of them snap off. There are screams and a terrible crash as BETTY hits the stage but we can't see anything even though the stage is still 'lit' by the footage of today's performance which is still running. It freezes on an audience member laughing. The image seems to burn off as if the projector has been left running. The variety bill on the other screen fades away like invisible ink.

Scene 10

When the lights return it is to the state in which the play began. The stage is stripped and the cinema screen has gone. HARVEY is alone in his opening position, only he's now holding a lasso, attached to nothing. It's like a noose. He looks devastated.

HARVEY: Sssssh. Sssssh. If you're quiet you can hear it. Listen. There, do you hear it? No? No. This is my place. This is my favourite place, like you have yours. Only there's been a mistake. Something went wrong, so I'm trapped; inside the walls, tied in the folds of the curtains and way, way up, floating next to the highest light. Because I didn't catch her. And that was my only job. To keep things running smoothly. To keep the show going. No-matter what. So I'm always here; a permanent fixture in this impermanent world. Waiting for Harry Lauder. Waiting for the change to come. The spice of life.

Harry Lauder's version of 'Keep Right On Till The End Of The Road' plays on throughout as each actor appears.

Scene 11

As the following information appears on the bill screen each character appears and stands on stage. This may be their bows, maybe not.

Enter CONNOR.

SCREEN: Connor McNair's screen test was a failure and

he never made a film. He did, however, become a household name during the 1940s, due to his appearances on the hit radio show, 'Goodtime Music'. During the war he travelled the world, entertaining troops, although he never engaged in battle. He settled in Australia, where he died in 1961. He never married.

Enter WALLY.

Wallace Shields – Dr Walford Chipo – was killed during the Second World War. He was in London on leave after his training for the Royal Navy, when a bomb hit his hotel. He was unscathed by the blast, but as he was helping a family escape from the rubble, the remainder of the roof gave way and he was crushed. The newspaper reports of the accident state that if it were not for Wally's 'unthinking bravery' the Liston Family, including their two children, would have perished.

Enter LORNA.

Lorna Singh enjoyed a long and successful career on the Scottish stage. Although records of her life are non-existent during the war years, she was still a fixture on variety bills well into the late '50s. The boom in superstition during the '40s saw her second on the bill in the Empire's 'Cavalcade' Christmas show, which, we must presume, was the highlight of her career.

Enter BETTY.

Betty Kemble's obituary stated that she died of 'heart problems', which in a way is true. She is remembered now as the composer of 'Me And My Man And The Moonlight' which is sung (in an ironic manner) by many modern female comic/singers on what remains of the variety circuit.

Enter JACK.

Jack Salt, devastated by the death of his wife, gave up show business altogether. He worked as a bookmaker, a travelling salesman and, at the time of his death in

1941, a baker. Jack is hard to find in records of the day, although his appearance in The Buchanan Footage, gives him some novelty value with music hall historians.

Enter CHARLIE.

After being sacked by Western Electrical Services, Charles Buchanan soon became a minor star. He was the first recorded comedian to 'spill out', that is to use light swearing and openly sexual references, now so common in stand up comics. This gave him a notoriety which eventually led to him becoming a fixture in pre-war Blackpool summer seasons. But it is his film footage of the King's last performance which keeps his name alive today. It is the only existing film footage of that style of variety and is vital to our understanding of the period. It now belongs to The British Library. Charlie died as a prisoner of war in 1943.

Enter EDWARD.

Three weeks after Betty's death, the clothes of Edward Todd were found on a beach in Ayrshire. He had been reported missing and was last seen heading for Lauder Ha', the famous residence of Harry Lauder, his hero. Whether he got there or spoke to Lauder is unknown. Certainly his name does not appear in Lauder's illustrious guest book. He is presumed to have drowned. An act of suicide.

Enter HARVEY.

The King's Theatre became the Regal Cinema on the thirteenth of February 1929. In 1978 it was converted into a Mecca bingo hall which closed in 1989. Today the building is derelict.

The End.

9 781840 023312